Faithful or Fearful?

Responding to the Politics of Fear

Charles Clemons

Faithful or Fearful?

Responding to the Politics of Fear

First Edition: 2025
Faithful or Fearful / Charles Clemons
ISBN: 978-1-969021-84-8 (Paperback)
ISBN: 978-1-969021-85-5 (Hardcover)
ISBN: 978-1-969021-86-2 (eBooks)

CONTENTS

"They're eating the dogs. They're eating the cats. They're eating the pets of the people that live there." [1,2]

Former 45th United States President, Donald Trump

~~~~~~~~~~~~~~~~~~~~~~~~~~~~~

"My Kingdom is not of this world."

Jesus

Political fear / (pə- 'li-ti-kəl 'fir) / *n*: The deliberate or unconscious use of fear to shape public opinion, control behavior, or maintain power within a political system. It involves invoking real or perceived threats—whether external (e.g., enemies, war) or internal (e.g., immigrants, minorities, dissenters)—to justify policies, suppress opposition, or rally support.

Example of political fear

On the evening of September 11, 2024, as I sat with friends watching the presidential election debate, we were fascinated to see the differences between the two candidates. One of the comments struck a nerve with us all. It was made by the former 45th president of the United States of America, Donald Trump. Amidst the melee of different views. On the economy. And on immigration, somewhere in the conversation. The former president echoed and amplified a statement made by his running mate for Vice President, J.D. Vance, that Haitian immigrants in Springfield, Ohio were eating the dogs, cats, and pets of its citizens.

Donald Trump used political fear when he portrayed the Haitians as a threat to public safety and culture. His words were used to rally support for his party and to justify stricter immigration controls and deportations.

---

[1] Catalini, Mike, et al. "Trump Falsely Accuses Immigrants in Ohio of Abducting and Eating Pets." AP News, 11 Sept. 2024, https://apnews.com/article/haitian-immigrants-vance-trump-ohio-6e4a47c52b23ae2c802d216369512ca5.

[2] Ray, Siladitya. "'They're Eating the Dogs' and 'Worst' Inflation: Key Fact-Checks from the Presidential Debate." *Forbes*, 11 Sept. 2024, https://www.forbes.com/sites/siladityaray/2024/09/11/theyre-eating-the-cats-and-worst-inflation-key-fact-checks-from-the-presidential-debate/.

Preface

Political fear is dangerous for Christians because it can replace faith with fear, love with suspicion, and truth with propaganda. Scripture often says, "Do not be afraid," not because the world is safe, but because God is in control, and fear should not dominate us.

Faithful or Fearful: Responding to the Politics of Fear is a response to fear-based manipulation of general masses of people for political gain. It is also an appeal to evangelical Christians to reconsider how political agendas may misrepresent their values, particularly in relation to actions and attitudes toward people who differ from them. I wrote this book to present an alternative way to respond to our turbulent times. Trusting in God's sovereignty allows us to recognize when fear is being used against us. Instead of isolating and criticizing those with different viewpoints, Scriptures and history show us enduring principles from those who stayed faithful to God in hard times. You can apply these principles to live without fear and to resist political manipulation.

This book challenges the political fears that may provoke you to see other people, such as Blacks, Whites, Asians, Latinos/Latinx, Immigrants, and Indigenous, as less than made in the image of God (Genesis 1:26). It also challenges you to confront these fears, encouraging you to move towards people who are different with curiosity, genuine interest, and the love of God and the Gospel of Jesus Christ (Matthew 11:22-37-39; 28:16-20). Doing so requires courage and honesty with ourselves.

Faithful or Fearful identifies the fear, provides clarifying definitions, presents Scripture that addresses the fear, and provides tools to help you starve the fear and feed the faith. We'll look at examples of how fear has been weaponized for political gain, and how Christ's followers can resist falling into that trap. We'll examine the antidote of the spiritual disciplines like prayer, Scripture reading, and community that can anchor us in the storm. And we'll unpack Jesus' radical ethic of enemy love, sacrificial service, and justice in unsettling times.

Chapter 1: Introduction

Fear is a powerful and primal emotion that has significant impact on human behavior. It is often described as an unpleasant feeling triggered by the perception of danger, real or imagined. Politics has risen to a position of significance among faith communities in the United States in recent years. When it comes to politics, fear can shape public opinion, influence policy decisions, and even determine the outcome of elections. Events have driven political fear into the lives of many Christians. To understand the politics of fear, it's essential to grasp the nature of fear and how it operates within the human psyche.

Political fear is the fear caused by political systems or authorities through violence, repression, exclusion, or propaganda, aimed at influencing behavior and suppressing opposition. It differs from political anxiety, which is concerned with one's commitment to a political course or the merits of an issue. Political fear has become significant enough in the lives of Christians that it has caused them to think and behave in ways that are inconsistent with their faith.

Politics is often called the skilled use of legitimate means to gain social control or to control society's resources, and fear has been used in societies to control the masses. The "politics of fear" is defined in the following ways:

- As a calculated use of fear to affect the behavior of a political body, ranging from an individual to a nation-state.
- As a political event that produces fear as a direct or unintended result, which can range from specific policies through international relations and war, to propaganda, rhetoric, and the actions of specific political figures.

Both concepts address fear's role as a motivator in politics. The politics of fear involves understanding how leaders use it as a tool for manipulation and how it restricts actions in such a way that victims may not fully grasp its impact.

The use of fear in politics is not a new phenomenon; it has been a function of human societies for centuries. History is replete with dictators and rebels who formed monumental national movements built on fear and hatred rather than the love of God in Christ Jesus, and each of those kingdoms fell like the ancient kingdoms foretold to Daniel in Babylon (Daniel 4).

Fear plays a significant role in politics, sociology, and global discussions. Researchers highlight the impact of fear on policymaking, community understanding, and political behavior. Notably, this research emerged after the 9/11 attacks that triggered fear on a massive scale. Despite its importance, fear remains relatively unexplored in political science, but understanding it can enhance our theories of political psychology.

The cycle of political fear

Before we get into a deeper discussion about the politics of fear, let's take a quick look at the cycle. In this section, you'll learn a little bit about the players, reactions, and actions associated with political fear.

The cycle begins with the delivery of a message intended to instill fear and animosity. When the message is publicized, people respond and take action. As you read this book, you'll see that the impact and consequences of political fear are complex and can be perpetuated throughout generations.

Note that there are many forms of political fear; this is just the basics.

The instigator delivers the message

The instigator, often a political figure or entity, communicates a message concerning a societal issue. The issue, whether actual or perceived, is frequently attributed to a particular group identified as scapegoats. The instigator relies on divisive tactics and exaggerated threats to gain support or create distractions from actual issues, causing public discord. Additionally, the message might emphasize that the instigator is the defender against the looming danger.

The instigator relies heavily on people who accept his message.

People hear and react

People who hear the message will have different emotions and reactions. Consider the reactions of following groups of people:

Submissive

The Submissive submit to the message and accept it. They view the danger as real and pressing, and they feel anger toward the scapegoats. They feel anxiety and dread related to the consequences that the Instigator predicts. They often look to the Instigator for protection and are willing to support any proposed fix.

Their fear? Well-being of themselves, their heirs, and their community due to the threat associated with the scapegoated people.

Resistant

The Resistant reject the message because it feels manipulative or exaggerated. They are annoyed and distrust the Instigator, framing larger systems as corrupt and dangerous. They also feel empathy and compassion for the scapegoated group of people.

Their fear? Systemic corruption, national discourse, and violence towards others.

Confused

The Confused aren't sure whether to believe the message or not. They can be swayed either way depending on who they trust.

Their fear? Maybe none until they align with either the Submissive or Resistant group of people.

Protective

The Protective, the group of scapegoats, feel personally attacked and often unsafe. They feel marginalized and have a sense of injustice, wondering why they are being blamed. This can result in shame or guilt as they internalize the blame. It can also result in a burning anger toward the attack on their integrity.

Their fear? Their livelihood, well-being, and even their lives.

People take action

After people hear the message and react, they begin to take action. Some actions can be immediate, and some might take time.

Submissive

The Submissive quickly take action to exclude the scapegoated group. They also resort to name-calling of the scapegoats and the Resistant group, labeling the Resistant as part of the problem.

They form public rallies to secure support from the Confused, and they show support toward the Instigator. They may issue threats or commit acts of violence, mobilizing any proposed fix, even if it's extreme.

Resistant

The Resistant may demonstrate a greater tendency to align with scapegoats, foster relationships, develop community backing, and advocate against perceived injustices. They push back publicly, fact-check, and distance themselves from the source. They organize public protests and demonstrations to gain support from the Confused. They also resort to name-calling of the Submissive and the Instigator.

Confused

The Confused might shut themselves off from social media to avoid the conflict altogether. If they are concerned about taking a stand, they might go to rallies that are organized by the Submissive and/or the Resistant.

Protective

The Protective, scapegoats, might silence themselves and withdraw from public life to avoid harm. Some of them might move to safer neighborhoods and/or build parallel communities where they feel safer. They develop a cultural pride as a source of dignity. They build unity by relying on support from family, religious groups, or the community. They may join in the demonstrations that the Resistant organize.

While some scapegoated individuals become resilient and resistant, others continue to internalize fear, potentially leading to challenges with mental health, generational distress, or disruptions within their communities.

Fear is perpetuated

Once the message is ingrained in members of society, the fear from all groups is passed down through the generations.

- The Instigator and successive leaders continue to perpetuate the message to heirs and to the growing number of Submissives.
- The Submissive perpetuate suspicion, prejudice, and superiority complexes to their heirs and communities. Laws and policies can reinforce stereotypes and impart the fear of the "other."
- The Resistant perpetuate their disdain for all those who align with the Instigator's message.
- The Protective scapegoats pass down stories of police raids and discrimination, warning children to "be careful." They learn to navigate spaces cautiously, shaping identity and behavior across generations.

The fears imposed are passed down throughout generations, and the division between the groups becomes more polarized.

Christian nationalism versus Christianity

Christian nationalism is a political ideology that merges Christian and nationalistic beliefs, often promoting the idea that the nation should be defined by its adherence to a particular interpretation of Christianity. This ideology can lead to exclusionary practices and policies, favoring one religious group over others and often marginalizing those who do not fit the nationalistic criteria. While the term "Christian nationalism" was coined in the 20th century, the mindset of identity politics and nationalism dates to biblical times.

Christianity, on the other hand, is a faith that's based on the teachings of Jesus Christ, emphasizing love, compassion, humility, and the salvation of all people. It is inclusive, welcoming individuals from all backgrounds and ethnicities. The core message of Christianity is found in the Great Commandment, *"Love the Lord your God with all your heart and with all your soul and with all your mind."* and *"Love your neighbor as yourself."* (Matthew 22:37-39).

Hotly debated issues may be held by your next-door neighbor or your own children. In discussing your faith or politics, you may feel defensive about your worldview as a Christian. This challenge is compounded by the fact that now, the emblems of your faith (the Cross and the Church) are so tightly associated with modern hate groups.

These hate groups include the individuals involved in the January 6th events at the Capitol Building—the Ku Klux Klan, the Proud Boys, the Oath Keepers, the Nazis—and past movements that used interpretations of Christianity to support slavery and territorial expansion.

The events on January 6th, reopened the wounds of deep-seated distrust and fear between White and Black people in America. Our long history of a racial divide between those communities was further deepened by the unfolding of an attempt to overthrow a certified United States election. And efforts towards racial harmony and Christian unity among the church were harmed with what appeared to be a parade of Christian nationalism in the capital of our country.

In the words of Amanda Tyler, leader of Christians Against Christian Nationalism Initiative, who described the events of January 6th, 2021:

"...white Christian nationalism and Christianity are not the same. The rioters who can accurately be labeled as radical Christian terrorists used Christianity as a mascot, trying to lend credibility and social acceptability to their terrorism. In the process, they sullied Christianity and Jesus in the hearts and minds of people all over the world."

Scapegoating and enemy creation

When a government uses political fear for manipulation and control, it typically involves scapegoating, or creating an enemy. A scapegoat is a person or group unfairly blamed for broader problems, such as economic struggles, disease, or social unrest. Scapegoating occurs through the monopolization of evil, where the ruling body attributes the existence of evil to a particular group or concept and then absolves others from it. It redirects attention from leaders or systemic issues to a target that is easier to address.

Enemy creation was evident during the Cold War era through McCarthyism when the U.S. government sought to eliminate communist influence by imposing anti-communist trials and tribunals. Anyone associated with communist countries was perceived as a threat, leading to prosecutions that ruined lives and careers, regardless of whether the accusations were true. Although communist ideology contradicts Christianity, these trials and the anti-communist movement exemplified political fear through enemy creation.

Christianity is often subject to marginalization when political fear is used by ruling governments. In such cases, the "enemy creation" process can occur as a form of manipulation and control. This occurs through the monopolization of evil, where the ruling body wishes to place the existence of evil onto someone or something, and then exonerates others from it. In doing so, the ruling government creates an enemy or inverse utopia that the government can use as a scapegoat should anything go wrong.

Conspiracy theories

A conspiracy theory is a theory that explains an event or set of circumstances as the result of a secret plot by usually powerful conspirators. A conspiracy theory often asserts that a secret of great importance is being kept from the public. Such was the case with the belief that getting the COVID-19 vaccine was tantamount to receiving the "mark of the Beast" as prophesied in Revelation 13:17.

Conspiracy theories and political fear are deeply intertwined, as fear often fuels the spread and belief in conspiracy theories. Political fear creates a psychological environment where conspiracy theories thrive, and conspiracy theories, in turn, increase political fear, creating a cycle that can shape public opinion and even influence policy decisions.

Us-versus-them mentality

Political fear divides people and makes them vulnerable to conspiracy theories, fostering distrust and hostility toward others.

Trends in immigration show increasing numbers of people of color entering the United States. This sparks fear for some people who fear a marked loss in birth rates among people of European ancestry. Negative attitudes towards foreigners also have risen as seen in hateful speech like, "Go back to your country!" or "Speak English!" or "They're taking our jobs away!" These sayings can be heard within local and national politics. And sadly, we must admit that the same kind of rants have been heard in the church.

At present, the theory of the Great Replacement fuels considerable anxiety among "White People" of European descent, who fear becoming a minority in America due to low birth rates and increased immigration from non-European regions such as Latin America, Asia, and Africa. This idea is compounded by historic caste systems in these regions, fostering an us-versus-them mentality.

In Black communities, there is a growing sense of nationalism where interracial dating and marriage are viewed as a betrayal of the race. Conversely, similar sentiments exist within some White communities, including the propagation of the "curse of Ham" myth to falsely justify racial segregation.

The discourse surrounding the Great Replacement Theory taps into long-standing anxieties and misconceptions about racial purity and social hierarchy. Martin Luther King Jr. once dreamt of a society where individuals are "judged by the content of their character, not the color of their skin." This vision challenges the divisive narratives that persist in both Black and White communities.

The Great Replacement Theory intertwines deeply with both historical and contemporary racial dynamics, urging a critical reassessment of our collective views on race and identity. For Christians, the Bible should be our ultimate guide, testing any philosophy against these questions: Is it true? Is it right? Does it align with the principles and teachings found in Scripture? How does it resonate with the life and teachings of Jesus Christ?

Unfortunately, this theory exploits a profound existential fear prevalent among many white Americans. However, it's worth remembering that one of the most frequently repeated commands in the Bible is "fear not," appearing nearly 365 times. A daily reminder to place trust in divine providence. By examining our beliefs and fears through the lens of Scripture, we can strive for a more inclusive and Christ-centered perspective, reflecting true faith and unity.

As W.E.B. Du Bois poignantly stated, "*The problem of the twentieth century is the problem of the color line.*" This quote reflects the enduring struggle against racial division and the fear of losing cultural identity.

Moreover, Frederick Douglass emphasized shared humanity in his speech, saying, *"If there is no struggle, there is no progress. Those who profess to favor freedom and yet depreciate agitation, are men who want crops without plowing up the ground."* This quote underscores the necessity of addressing these fears and prejudices to achieve true progress.

Examples of political fear

Fear is an unpleasant and often strong emotion caused by the anticipation or awareness of danger. This anticipatory awareness often causes people to be irrational and do things beyond the norm, which is bad for society. In being irrational, people don't or won't think things critically and carefully, and the results of their actions might be damaging to themselves and others.

While there are abundant examples of political fear, you'll see through the following short examples that the origins and outcome of political fear can be varied.

Authoritarian powers: 1800s – 1900s

Authoritarians Hitler, Stalin, and Napoleon all stimulated fear to control society. Their actions brought fear to the international arena by generating the fear not only of war against other countries to gain more power and control, but also by creating the image of an infallible leader. Their administrations used fear as a tool not only against enemies, but of what would happen without them.

It's the same case in modern politics where fear is often used as a tool to mobilize support or to suppress opposition. Some political leaders and parties exploit fears related to economic instability, social change, or external threats to rally their base or to justify controversial policies.

Terrorism: September 11, 2001

The 9/11 attacks serve as a significant illustration of how political fear can be both triggered by an event and subsequently used for political purposes. The event of the 9/11 attacks have caused a great deal of fear in American society.

This fear caused many Americans to have xenophobia against Muslims, and they have done things beyond the norm, such as abusing innocent Muslims in Western countries. In response to the massive influx of immigrants from other countries, namely Latin America, as well as the Caribbean, and Africa, the cry is "Go back to ..." The real or perceived threats of violence become a justification to exact cruelty on those who are here illegally or are unwanted.

Though the issues of managing the security and safety of a nation's border and using its limited resources for citizenry are factual concerns, fear-driven responses move people to react quickly in ways that might be without justice, mercy, or humility.

Political discord: current day, 2025

Consider the extreme reactions that the political right and left have toward one another and their different vision for America in our current day. Many Americans live in communities separate from people with whom they disagree and have no basis of relationship to have meaningful dialogue or debate. Instead, out of fear, shouting matches occur at town hall meetings, and political debates held by officials of the highest office in the United States. These actions are a far cry from the way of Jesus Christ.

America's top fears

Political fear, whether real or manufactured, can perpetuate and intensify fears about disease, death, and corruption. In turn, these fears deepen political divisions, reduce trust in institutions, and create a population more prone to conspiracy thinking and reactionary politics. This cycle keeps people on edge, making them more vulnerable to manipulation by those who benefit from fear-driven narratives.

As you read further, you'll learn about some of the top fears of Americans based on research, examples of some of those fears, and how Christians can address them. Additionally, you'll get information about research on desires.

Recent research on fears

We live in turbulent and anxious times, with many people feeling a sense of dread or apprehension about the future. As you read the following recent survey results about fear and anxiety, consider what David reminds us, *"God is our refuge and strength, a very present help in trouble."* (Psalm 46:1).

In 2024, approximately 18.2% of U.S. adults reported experiencing symptoms of anxiety. This represents a significant increase from previous years, with rates rising from 15.6% in 2019 to 18.2% in 2022. Young adults, particularly those aged 18-29, were the most affected, with 26.6% reporting anxiety symptoms.[3]

Chapman University (CU) conducts yearly surveys on American fears. What has been previously described anecdotally has been researched and quantified by CU. These specialists have discussed fear and compiled a list by percentages of their sample population studied.

One survey compiled a list of American fears. The topics compiled for 2022 cover a range of concerns.[4] The following table shows a sample of notable fears:

Top Fears of 2022	% Afraid
1. Corrupt government officials	79.6
2. Government restrictions on firearms	48.9
3. Global warming and climate change	48.7
4. White supremacists	43.4
5. Random mass shootings	36.7

The same Chapman University research shows Americans' uppermost fears (being afraid or very afraid). The survey states, "These are scary times, and it is understandable why people are frightened!" It also indicates that a hyper-patriotism for America now clashes with a hyper-hatred against America, so much so that citizens who have clear differences of opinion are unable to hold a conversation with civility. This growing animosity appears to resonate from people identifying with their political party more than as children of God. It's as if only a "win-lose" mindset has gripped the country.

[3] Mundell, E. (2024, November 7). *Rates of Anxiety, Depression Rising Among Americans, Especially the Young.* Usnews.com. https://www.usnews.com/news/health-news/articles/2024-11-07/rates-of-anxiety-depression-rising-among-americans-especially-the-young

[4] "America's Top 10 Fears: The 2021 American Fear Index." Safehome.org, www.safehome.org/home-safety/american-fear-study/. Accessed 29 Dec. 2022.

The following table shows the compiled statistics drawn from the national survey:

Top Fears of 2022	% Afraid or Very Afraid
1. Corrupt government officials	62.1
2. People I love becoming seriously ill	60.2
3. Russia using nuclear weapons	59.6
4. People I love dying	58.1
5. The U.S. becoming involved in world war	56.0
6. Pollution of drinking water	54.5
7. Not having enough money for the future	53.7
8. Economic/financial collapse	53.7
9. Pollution of oceans, rivers, and lakes	52.5
10. Biological warfare	51.5

Examples of our top fears

As you read the following examples related to Americans' top fears, you'll see that the fears invoked by a circumstance are not isolated, but very much connected. For example, with the COVID-19 pandemic, we saw fear of government control, fear of disease, and fear of those who are different.

Fear of government corruption

These are scary times, and it is understandable why people are frightened. As of February 5, 2023, 1.1 million people in the United States of America had died from COVID-19. Depending on your point of view, the coronavirus may be a non-issue for you.

For some people, a major concern was the thought of a secret government conspiracy to control the masses. For some in the United States, to take the "vaccine" was tantamount to receiving the "mark of the Beast" as prophesied in Revelation 13:17. And for anyone who believed they acquiesced to such a thing would be horrible!

Fear of disease

The intersection of political fear and disease occurs more often than expected. Consider the HIV/AIDS crisis in the 1980s that first drew public attention within gay communities. It resulted in a response driven by homophobia and moral panic.

Some conservative politicians used AIDS to push moral agendas, calling for restrictions on gay rights, immigrants, or sex education. Plans such as tracking lists, quarantine, and required testing mixed fear of disease with political control.

Politicians and media often characterized it as a "gay disease," fostering an us-versus-them mentality. This fear contributed to stigma, rejection, and discrimination against individuals affected by the virus.

Fear of those who are different

Fear, hatred, and political rancor is growing. To disagree with your political opponent is to label them as "Evil," "Marxist," or "Fascist" (whether they are or not). Labels are easy to use and are often poorly defined and further misunderstood. It's easy to call someone a "racist," a "Marxist," "a Liberal," or a "Right-Wing Bigot." For anyone, pejorative labels don't build bridges toward a civil conversation. For Christians specifically, name-calling poorly represents the life of Jesus Christ and how he engaged people, even his opponents and enemies.

For many in the Black community, a sense of despair, hopelessness, and profound cynicism toward the larger White community has been borne from the pain of previous generations of injustice and present-day brutality towards their community. Consequently, a mass exodus of Blacks from many multi-ethnic churches has occurred with some either returning to predominantly Black churches or dropping church attendance completely. This migration includes many young people across all ethnic groups who feel disillusioned with a segregated church that mirrors the legal segregation of the 50s and 60s, yet has leaders who yielded to nationalistic rhetoric that smacks of racism.

Fear of economic and financial collapse

With the increasing division of the nation along political party lines and the occasional violent demonstrations, fear continues to rise. The division is costly, and the effects are the inability to agree on how to manage our national economy. Economic uncertainties contribute to the undercurrent of fear as well.

Our looming national debt and potential financial collapse cause people to fear for the future of their children. Some people have a lingering feeling of scarcity. A fear that what we have will run out! A frantic fear of poverty. What's going to happen to my children? My grandchildren? Does America have enough to go around? Who is American? And how much should we share with those not born in the U.S.A.? People with these kinds of questions and this kind of thinking look with suspicion toward immigrants and/or foreigners. A sense of falling behind, fear of inadequate retirement funds, or concern for children's future can motivate people to take action. The concern of being left behind, coupled with the fear of insufficient retirement funds or limited opportunities for future generations, can motivate individuals to take action.

Fear of climate change

If you're not concerned about the financial challenges of the U.S., you might be concerned about the state of the planet, such as climate change. Consider the divide that we have within the United States. Progressives fear ecological collapse and rally support for green policies while conservatives fear that policy changes will take away our freedom, our jobs, and our cars. Even if you think climate change is a hoax, it is a topic of debate that influences the political views of many in the country.

Fear of international crisis

Added to our list of national woes are the ominous threats of foreign actors from enemy countries who sow division through social media and other communications to pit one American against another, including the battle between genders too.

What Americans desire

With so many people without hope and struggling to find a sense of peace, it's no surprise that we see frequencies of suicide, mass shootings, gun violence, divorce, and workplace burnout. The deep longing of many in America is to survive the turbulent times in which we live.

A research study by the Barna Group (a Christian public opinion research company) discovered that more than a third of adults and teens (13-

17 years of age) are seeking inner peace (37%), hope (35%), and healing and forgiveness (30%) in their spiritual beliefs.

How Christians can respond

For those who follow the "Prince of Peace" (Isaiah 9:6), many people want to know if Christians are aware of their desperate needs and if the Church cares enough to help. How will the message of the Gospel of Jesus Christ be delivered to people who are fearful of and/or frustrated with Christians? And how is the Christian to love his neighbor when living with the above fears?

In studying the role of fear in politics, it's essential to consider the influence of Christians both historically and currently. The beliefs and values of leaders, interest groups, and voters shape political culture.

Far too often, professing Christians act in ways that resemble Jonah. Consider the story of the Prophet in Jonah 1-4 where we read that Jonah was called by God to bring a message of repentance to the people of Nineveh. Jonah was so grieved that God would show compassion towards people he saw as enemies that he chose go to other parts of the world instead of delivering the message that would ultimately save thousands of lives. The story of Jonah and the lesson of compassion that the LORD taught him serves as an allegory for the American Church in today's turbulent society.

With the increasing political involvement of many Christians, there is also a rise in embittered and angry treatment of others. This is evident in a reticent attitude towards people who are different and people who are in need from different backgrounds. Just as Jonah cared only for his comfort and was ignorant of the peril of the sailors who were taking care of him, highly politically involved Christians often ignore or curse their political opponents rather than seek their well-being. While these generalizations do not apply to all professing Christians involved in politics, they do apply to many who see their political opponents as enemies unworthy of care, empathy, and genuine love as fellow human beings made in the image of God.

In secular societies, religion has limited influence, but in Western countries such as New Zealand and the United States, evangelical Christians shape cultural trends and discussions. It's important to consider their outlook on fear and its use in politics as it has the potential to profoundly impact the greater community. So, how do Christians perceive fear? How should they address it? And what potential do they have to influence change in fear-laden political climates?

Live in hope

Without God, there is plenty to fear in this world full of troubles. Yet, Jesus Christ made a promise to His followers, *"I have told you these things so that in me you may have peace. In this world, you will have trouble. But take heart! I have overcome the world."* (John 16:33). Jesus Christ gives hope that fortifies the Christian against the waves of trials and sorrows that crash into our lives. And even more, to thrive abundantly (John 10:10) by pursuing His purpose for us knowing that *"God causes all things to work for good, to those who love God, to those who are called according to His purpose."* (Romans 8:18-28).

The threat to life previously mentioned becomes an opportunity to display His life in us by the Spirit. Living in hope and peace through an active relationship with God will strengthen you against fear. Further, when the Christian endures hardships as a soldier of Christ, we are developed in character that is resilient and able to comfort those who would face similar trying situations (2 Corinthians 1:3-4).

Embrace the spirit of love, power, and self-control

God reminds us of what He gives to His children. *"God has not given you a spirit of fear, but love, power, and self-control."* (2 Timothy 1:7). These words were given by the Apostle Paul to his adopted son in ministry, Timothy. Paul reminded him that God gave him the ability to fulfill his Christian duties as a minister to the Church in Ephesus. The city of Ephesus was full of idolatry, immorality, and Roman brutality. It became hostile to the presence of Christians because of their negative impact on the idol market (Acts 19:26-28). So much so that the coppersmiths and craftsmen guild rioted to run the Apostle Paul out of the city (2 Timothy 4:14). Timothy was prone to be a bit fearful, nervous, and even timid.

The early Christians faced an intensity of persecution unfamiliar to the American Church today. To the reader, you too may experience different forms of fear as well when it comes to making known that you are a follower of Jesus Christ. We are cautioned about a fear that would deny Christ:

"The statement is trustworthy: For if we died with Him, we will also live with Him; If we endure, we will also reign with Him; If we deny Him, He will also deny us; If we are faithless, He remains faithful, for He cannot deny Himself. (2 Timothy 2:11–13).

We who place our faith in Christ, like Timothy, need to be reminded that God has not given His children a "spirit of cowardice," but "love, power, and self-control." (2 Timothy 1:7). Some may bristle at this charge, saying "I'm not afraid of anything or anyone." For a few individuals, that may be true to a degree. But generally, fear is very present in our society. Watching nightly news broadcasts or watching live footage can provoke a response. These kinds of fears can also be weaponized or used as a tool toward specific ends.

If God hadn't given Timothy a "spirit of fear" (v.7), I wonder who or what did. Have you ever asked, "What am I afraid of?" As a tool, fear within politics holds sway over the decisions we make, including where you live, where you work, the friends you have, where you worship, your view of your country, your view of other nationalities, your view of the present, and your view of the future for your children and yourself. If we are honest, fear can touch any of the previous things mentioned and drive us to make decisions not rooted in the love, power, or self-control of God but knee-jerk reactions that rarely solve problems but create greater divisions and animosity among people.

Remember that Jesus is our rock

When was the last time you heard a political or ministry leader humbly confess their fears? Can you recall someone saying, "I'm afraid about the future of our children;" I am afraid that our country is on the brink of collapse;" or "I fear for the lives of my children when they drive."? Maybe you have heard these statements?

Possibly with a call to turn back to God in repentance, to pray for God's guidance and protection with faith in Jesus Christ. This is needed much like the repentance of Nineveh at the preaching of Jonah (Jonah 4). Instead of blaming or insulting others, a greater solution is to confess your fears to God, repent of your sin, and turn towards His word for guidance in how to live and respond towards fear.

The good news is that we can come to God's word for the stability we need to face the storms of life. Are you afraid? Do you feel nervous about the present and future? It's okay, Timothy was too. Today, place your complete confidence in Jesus Christ through repentance and faith. Believing that He not only died for your sins, and rose again, but He promises to never leave you. He said,

> *"Therefore everyone who hears these words of mine and puts them into practice is like a wise man who built his house on the rock. The rain came down, the streams rose, and the winds blew and beat against that house; yet it did not fall, because it had its foundation on the rock. But everyone who hears these words of mine and does not put them into practice is like a foolish man who built his house on sand. The rain came down, the streams rose, and the winds blew and beat against that house, and it fell with a great crash."* (Matthew 5:24-27).

Jesus Christ, the Master Teacher, told this parable when He taught the Sermon on the Mount (Matthew 5-7). His message was not only to hear his words but also to do them. Two men, both heard, but their responses were linked to their destinies. One obeyed, the other did not. But both faced storms, the house of one stood, while the other collapsed. Are you fearful of the present storms? Are you fearing vaccines and conspiracies? Far-Right Extremists? Far-Left Extremists? If yes, there is good news! Because Jesus Christ remains true to His promise that His word is rock! By His enablement to love, power, and self-control we can respond right to the politics of fear.

Chapter 2: The politics of fear

The sources of political fear are numerous and diverse. The COVID-19 pandemic upended life as we knew it, with over 1.1 million American deaths, economic disruptions, and debates over vaccine mandates and government overreach. Increasing political polarization has Americans bitterly divided along partisan lines, struggling to hold civil conversations and see the humanity in those they disagree with.

Racial tensions also simmer. Some people fear the impacts of changing demographics while those in minority communities feel disillusioned by the enduring legacy of discrimination and injustice. It's been said that the January 6th Capitol riots "reopened the wounds of deep-seated distrust and fear between White and Black people in America."

Diverging values and worldviews also cause trepidation, noting that there is a "frantic fear of poverty... Who is American? And how much should we share with those not born in the U.S.A.?" These kinds of questions and this kind of thinking look with suspicion toward immigrants and/or foreigners.

In such an environment of angst, people can be driven to irrational thoughts and actions out of fear. When individuals act irrationally, they fail to consider matters critically and thoroughly, potentially leading to harmful outcomes for themselves and others. Fear can breed hatred, suspicion of outgroups, and a win-lose, zero-sum mentality. In other words, when fearful and not faithful to Jesus Christ's way of seeing and treating people, foreigners can be viewed as taking something from those born in a nation.

How to identify political fear

It's important to be able to identify political fear. Voices and messages from instigators might seem innocuous to you, particularly if you're not really interested or affected by the fear that's being imposed. But listen closely, observe, and ask yourself questions for some signs of political fear.

- **The message drives division instead of unity.** Messaging or leadership uses fear of "the other" to gain support. **Ask** if the message is prompting you to love your neighbor less. Remember John's words, *"There is no fear in love; but perfect love casts out fear, because fear involves torment."* (1 John 4:18).

- **The message fuels injustice.** Policies or attitudes lead to exclusion or discrimination. **Ask** if the position reflects justice, mercy, and humility. Note the words of the prophet Micah, *"What does the Lord require of you? To act justly and to love mercy..."* (Micah 6:8).

- **The message promotes idolatry of nation or party.** Political parties and national identity are viewed as the highest expressions of authority. **Ask** if your hope is in Christ's return or in saving a country through political governance. Remember that Paul tells us *"Our citizenship is in heaven."* (Philippians 3:20).

- **The message distorts the Church's mission.** Church communities might prioritize political ideologies over religious teachings. **Ask** if you're trusting political power more than God's kingdom.

Generally, if you hear someone constantly warning of danger, pointing fingers, and insisting only they can save you, you're likely seeing political fear in action. The Christian response is to remain anchored in Christ's peace, guided by truth, and committed to love and justice.

Historical contexts of fear in politics

Throughout history, leaders have used fear to control populations and maintain power.

One of the most notorious examples is Adolf Hitler, who leveraged fears of economic hardship, political instability, and ethnic minorities to consolidate his power in Germany. His propaganda machine spread fear and hatred, leading to the atrocities of World War II and the Holocaust.

Similarly, Joseph Stalin used fear to maintain his grip on the Soviet Union. Through purges, show trials, and a pervasive secret police force, Stalin instilled fear in his citizens, ensuring compliance and eliminating dissent. The fear of being labeled an enemy of the state led many to betray friends and family, highlighting the destructive power of fear.

Napoleon Bonaparte also used fear to consolidate power and expand his empire. By portraying himself as a defender of France against external threats and internal chaos, he justified his authoritarian rule. His military campaigns spread fear across Europe, reshaping the continent's political landscape.

In modern times, fear continues to play a crucial role in politics. The aftermath of the 9/11 attacks in the United States saw a significant increase in the politics of fear. The threat of terrorism became a central theme in American political discourse, leading to the invasion of Iraq and the implementation of policies such as the Patriot Act. These actions were justified by the need to protect national security, but they also raised concerns about civil liberties and the abuse of power. One of the more recent examples of political fear points to Vladimir Putin who's weaving a narrative of Russia being threatened by Western aggression to justify his brutal attacks on Ukraine.

Examples: The use of fear in contemporary politics

Consider the following examples that illustrate the impact of fear in contemporary politics:

- **The war on terror.** After the 9/11 attacks, the U.S. government used the fear of terrorism to garner public support for military interventions in Afghanistan and Iraq. The fear of another terrorist attack was a driving force behind policies that expanded executive power and curtailed civil liberties.

- **Immigration and xenophobia.** In many Western countries, fear of immigration has been used to justify restrictive policies and harsh rhetoric. Political leaders often depicted immigrants as threats to national security, economic stability, and cultural identity. This fear has fueled xenophobia and discrimination, leading to policies that separate families and create hostile environments for migrants.

- **Populist movements.** Populist leaders around the world have used fear of elites, globalization, and cultural change to rally support. By positioning themselves as defenders of the common people against a corrupt establishment, these leaders exploit fear to gain power and to implement their agendas. This has led to increased polarization and division within societies.

Faith in action: Shining examples of Christian living

Throughout history, there have been remarkable examples of individuals living out their Christian faith, often in stark contrast to the fear and bigotry seen in certain segments of society today. These modern-day challenges echo the mixed emotions and struggles faced by the ancient and medieval church.

Defending the faith in the face of persecution

The Apostolic Father Polycarp is a shining example of unwavering faith. In his defense of Christianity, he articulated how the Christian faith was beneficial to Roman society and not inherently seditious. Polycarp made this defense even as he faced execution by Roman officials.

Instead of resorting to violence, many Christians throughout history have followed the teachings of Jesus Christ, as found in Matthew 5:16-17, by letting their light shine through good works that glorify God. These actions of love and service have been the true method of spreading the Christian faith, rather than through force or government mandates, as seen in Roman Emperor Constantine's attempts. The Great Commission, found in Matthew 28:16-20, underscores the importance of spreading the Gospel through service and proclamation.

Acts of service during persecution

The legacy of Christian service during times of persecution is well-documented. One such instance is the care of the sick and dying during plagues and famines. Eusebius of Caesarea recorded that Christians in Caesarea cared for the dying, buried the dead, and distributed bread to those weakened by famine. Their deeds were widely praised, highlighting their commitment to service.

Another notable example is the hospitality and charity demonstrated by early Christians who provided food, shelter, and care for the poor and needy, often at great personal risk. This practice was so notable that even the last Pagan emperor, Julian the Apostate, acknowledged that Christian charity significantly contributed to the spread of Christianity. Today, organizations like the Salvation Army continue this tradition of Christian service, providing aid to those in need.[5],[6]

Acts of compassion and service

Early Christians rescued abandoned babies from a common practice of infanticide in ancient Rome. By raising these infants as their own, they provided powerful testimony to their faith and love for their neighbors. This tradition continues today with various service centers and pregnancy resource centers offering support to young mothers and fathers.

Hospitality to the poor is a hallmark of Christian service. Early Christians opened their homes to travelers and the needy, offering food, shelter, and support. This tradition, rooted in the teachings of Jesus and the apostles, continues today in urban areas with homeless shelters, crisis centers, and places where people can find a hot meal and feel loved.[7]

Caring for lepers is another example of Christian service. Christians often provided food, medical care, and companionship to those suffering from leprosy, demonstrating their commitment to serving the marginalized.

These compassionate responses contrast sharply with the fearful and exclusionary actions seen during the early years of the HIV/AIDS crisis in the 1980s. Some American churches viewed HIV/AIDS as a curse and retreated from those affected. However, many Christian communities resisted this impulse and reflected the love of Jesus in their actions.

Modern-day challenges

Sadly, many people in the American Church today bow to fear and are exploited by corrupt political leaders who promise prosperity in exchange for exclusivity, isolationism, and aggression toward outsiders. This stands in stark contrast to the examples of faithful service seen throughout history. True Christian charity cares for all people from the womb to the tomb,

---

[5] Eusebius of Caesarea, *Ecclesiastical History*

[6] Julian the Apostate, *Letters*

[7] Early Christian Writings, *The Apostolic Fathers*

embracing a holistic approach to love and service that transcends political divides.

Unscrupulous politicians and leaders have proven skilled at capitalizing on these fears for their own gain using the politics of fear, a calculated use of fear to affect the behavior of a political body. "If I can make you afraid, cause a large stir, or create panic among people, by fear, you and those around you can be manipulated into action." Sounds sinister? It is.

As Christians, how are we to respond to such a climate of fear, anger, and division? Remember the reassuring words of Jesus, *"In this world you will have trouble. But take heart! I have overcome the world."* (John 16:33). Though we will face trials and persecutions, we can find peace and hope in Christ, who reminds us *"God has not given you a spirit of fear, but of power, love and self-discipline."* (2 Timothy 1:7).

Rather than being controlled by our fears and anxieties, we are called to put our ultimate trust in God's sovereign wisdom and build our lives on the solid foundation of His truth. As Jesus taught:

> *"Everyone who hears these words of mine and puts them into practice is like a wise man who built his house on the rock. The rain came down, the streams rose, and the winds blew and beat against that house; yet it did not fall, because it had its foundation on the rock."* (Matthew 7:24-25).

This radical trust and obedience to Christ provides an unshakable mooring amid the storms of life. It frees us from making rash or regrettable decisions rooted in fear, hate, or self-preservation. Instead, we can operate from a position of wisdom, courage, and Christ-like love for others, including our perceived enemies or those with whom we disagree.

To be clear, having fears is an understandable part of the human experience. Even the Apostle Paul's protégé, Timothy, struggled with fear and timidity, which is why Paul reminded him, *"God has not given us a spirit of fear..."* (2 Timothy 1:7). Jesus' disciples also expressed fears during scary circumstances like storms at sea."

The key is to not let those fears control us or cause us to act in ways that dishonor God and dehumanize others who are made in His image. This book examines biblical principles aimed at addressing divisive political fears that foster animosity, and provides guidance for individuals to act as responsible citizens grounded in Christ's love, truth, and enduring values.

The path will not always be easy or comfortable. But has any follower of Jesus been promised an easy road? As we'll see, the Church has sometimes taken positions that differ from prevailing cultural norms, standing up to unjust fear-mongers and demagogues at great risk. But ultimately, our hope is not in any political personality or platform, but in the unshakable Kingdom of our risen Lord.

So take heart—though the waves of cultural fear may swell, we were made for such a time as this. Now is our opportunity to be lighthouses shining the radiant truth and love of Christ into the darkness and tumult around us. Let us walk this journey side by side, without fear.

Scriptural insights on fear

The Bible offers profound insights into the nature of fear and how believers should respond to it. Throughout Scripture, God's people are often admonished not to fear.

God reassures His people saying, *"So do not fear, for I am with you; do not be dismayed, for I am your God. I will strengthen you and help you; I will uphold you with my righteous right hand."* (Isaiah 41:10).

Jesus frequently tells His followers not to be afraid, saying, *"Do not be afraid of those who kill the body but can't kill the soul. Rather, be afraid of the One who can destroy both soul and body in hell."* (Matthew 10:28). This teaching highlights the importance of placing our fear and trust in God rather than in earthly powers or threats.

The apostle Paul also addresses fear in his letters. He writes, *"For God has not given us a spirit of timidity, but of power and love and discipline."* (2 Timothy 1:7). This verse encourages believers to rely on the Holy Spirit for strength and courage in the face of fear.

Theological reflections on fear and faith

Fear and faith are often depicted as opposing forces in the Christian life. While fear can paralyze and enslave, faith empowers and liberates. Theologically, fear is seen as a result of humanity's fallen state, while faith is a gift from God that enables believers to trust in His promises and act courageously.

Understanding the theological principles concerning fear can empower the Christian in a right response to fear. Understanding that God rules, has a plan, and can use or redeem suffering for His eternal purposes can empower a person not to fold to the trappings of fear.

The story of David and Goliath (1 Samuel 17) is a powerful example of faith overcoming fear. Despite the immense size and strength of Goliath, David's faith in God gave him the courage to face the giant. An aspect of David's faith was completely opposite of his countrymen and his own king Saul. In some ways David's fight of faith was a political fight to not go along with the crowd who feared Goliath more than God. His victory was not just a triumph of skill or bravery, but a testament to the power of faith in God.

In the New Testament, the early Christians faced persecution and martyrdom. Yet, their faith in the resurrection and the hope of eternal life gave them the strength to endure suffering and remain steadfast. The book of Revelation, written to encourage persecuted believers, repeatedly calls for patient endurance and faithfulness, reminding them of the ultimate victory of Christ.

Practical applications: Navigating fear in political life

As Christians, navigating fear in political life requires discernment, wisdom, and a reliance on God's guidance. Consider the following practical guidelines:

- **Stay informed.** Educate yourself about political issues and the ways fear is being used to influence public opinion. Understanding the facts can help you discern between legitimate concerns and fearmongering.
- **Pray for discernment.** Ask God for wisdom and discernment to see through fear-based rhetoric and to respond in a manner that reflects His love and justice.

- **Engage in dialogue.** Foster open and respectful conversations with people who hold different political views. This can help break down barriers of fear and build mutual understanding.
- **Promote peace and justice.** Advocate for policies and actions that promote peace, justice, and the common good. Stand against fear-based policies that harm vulnerable populations.
- **Trust in God.** Remember that ultimate security comes from God, not from political leaders or policies. Place your trust in His sovereignty and faithfulness.

Chapter 3: Address scapegoating and embrace diversity

As I write this book, after many revisions, we have witnessed numerous instances of suspicion and scapegoating in our society. One such example occurred during the 2024 Presidential debate, where the former United States President accused Haitian immigrants of eating the dogs, cats, and pets of citizens of Springfield, Ohio. This baseless accusation not only fueled xenophobia but also perpetuated harmful stereotypes about immigrants.

Years earlier, during her campaign for President in 2016, the former Secretary of State made a sweeping generalization about political conservatives who supported Donald Trump. She stated:

> *"You know, to be grossly generalistic, you could put half of Trump's supporters into what I call the basket of deplorables. Right? [Laughter/applause]. The racist, sexist, homophobic, xenophobic, Islamophobic — you name it. And unfortunately, there are people like that. And he has lifted them up. He has given voice to their websites that used to only have 11,000 people and now have eleven million. He tweets and retweets offensive, hateful, mean-spirited rhetoric. Now some of those folks, they are irredeemable, but thankfully they are not American."*

She went on to express that the other half of Trump's supporters were desperate Americans seeking change due to legitimate concerns about the economy, factory closures, food insecurity, and the opioid crisis. However, such generalizations by politicians often drive negative relationships within the community.

As Christians, we have an opportunity to use our words to unite and heal, even while speaking the truth in love. The way to overcome evil suspicions is by getting to know people and forming genuine relationships. When Jesus Christ visited the woman at the well in John 4, He crossed many religious, cultural, and social bridges to meet with her and transform her life. Are we willing to do the same?

Scapegoating entrapments

It's a tragic pattern that has repeated itself throughout human history when majority groups see minority populations as potential enemies to be feared rather than neighbors to be embraced. The dominant culture, often spurred on by power-hungry leaders and populist fearmongering, generates anxiety over the "other" and takes draconian measures to oppress them, setting the stage for atrocities.

We see this in countless examples, from the brutalities of Indigenous peoples at the hands of European colonialists who suspected them of being subhuman savages, to the Nazis' insidious propaganda painting Jews as rats and vermin that endangered the future of the Reich, ultimately leading to the Holocaust's horrors. In more recent times, we've seen it in the United States with the internment of Japanese Americans during World War II due to racist suspicions that they could not be trusted and might betray the nation from within.

The consequences of such detrimental suspicion extend beyond the affected groups, influencing entire societies and nations. This erosion of principles can lead to widespread injustice and self-inflicted challenges. An atmosphere of distrust and division takes root, preventing the cultivation of the pluralistic harmony and cultural exchange that has been the source of human civilization's greatest achievements when we've learned to embrace our diversity rather than fear it.

Psychologists have studied how the human mind can easily fall into the trap of unconscious bias, stereotyping, and prejudice toward outgroups perceived as threatening or fundamentally "other." Unfortunately, our brains tend toward building walls instead of bridges if we allow our worst impulses toward tribalism and zero-sum thinking to go unchecked. Fear of the unfamiliar can quickly curdle into moral exclusion and justify the unjustifiable.

Biblical guidance on treating those who are different

As Christians, we are not immune from the tendency toward suspicion and prejudice. Too often, Church history is marred by examples when professing believers allowed cultural blinders to shape their perspective more than the radically inclusive ethic that Christ modeled. We forget that Jesus prompted outrage simply by sharing a meal and dialogue with those who the religious elite had pre-judged as irredeemable sinners and traitors. He placed a premium on seeing people made in God's image first rather than through superficial cultural lenses. Consider the biblical instructions for embracing inclusivity.

Keep focused on the truth of the Gospel

In 1 Timothy 6, the Apostle Paul addresses a faction within the Church that had given in to what he describes as people with "corrupt minds" who traffic in "evil suspicions and constant friction."

This was likely a group that had allowed cultural prejudices to fester within their understanding of the life of faith. Their constant "controversies and quarrels about words" stemmed from an "unhealthy interest" that had allowed them to become consumed by biases, rumors, and side controversies that distracted them from the truth of the Gospel.

Practice the renewal of your mind

Paul's antidote is to insist on "sound instruction" that reflects the teachings of Christ. Elsewhere in Scripture, we are commanded to *"not be conformed to the patterns of this world but be transformed by the renewing of your mind."* (Romans 12:2). In other words, we must actively resist the toxic thought patterns and evil suspicions that are so prevalent in the fallen world. We can't afford to remain oblivious to our tendencies toward prejudice or be shaped by the fear-mongering voices that seek to turn us against our neighbors.

The renewal of our minds occurs through immersing in the truths of Scripture, engaging with a community of believers who can lovingly hold us accountable, and modeling our thoughts and perspectives after those of Christ. When Jesus saw the ethnic Samaritan woman drawing water from a well, he didn't allow the natural suspicion between their people groups at the time to cloud his vision. Instead, he offered her the living water of salvation and drew her into a revelatory dialogue that shattered cultural barriers.

Avoid cultural prejudices

When the disciples sought to turn away the mothers trying to bring their children for Jesus' blessing, he rebuked them sternly. Again and again, Jesus challenged those around him—including his closest followers—to reject their culture's prejudices and see people as God sees them rather than through lenses of suspicion, fear, or moral exclusion.

Ultimately, the life of Christ exemplified the truth that *"there is neither Jew nor Greek, neither slave nor free, neither male nor female"* in the Kingdom of God (Galatians 3:28). The boundaries and suspicions erected by worldly tribalism and prejudice are deconstructed in those who have truly been transformed by the Spirit into citizens of God's coming Kingdom on earth as it is in heaven. It's a radical, upside-down vision where all are welcomed as equals in the Beloved Community.

Love those who are different

In Deuteronomy 10:12-22, the Bible emphasizes the importance of loving and serving God wholeheartedly and extending that love and justice to others, especially those who are vulnerable and marginalized. The passage begins by outlining what God requires of the Israelites: to fear Him, walk in His ways, love Him, and serve Him with all their heart and soul. It highlights God's sovereignty over all creation and His special affection for the Israelites, chosen from among all peoples. However, this chosen status comes with a responsibility. The Israelites are called to "circumcise their hearts," meaning they must be humble and obedient, not stubborn. They are instructed to love foreigners:

> *"He defends the cause of the fatherless and the widow and loves the foreigner residing among you, giving them food and clothing. And you are to love those who are foreigners, for you yourselves were foreigners in Egypt."* (Deuteronomy 10:18-19).

This passage reminds us that God's love and justice extend to all people, regardless of their background or status. As Christians, we are called to follow this example by treating foreigners and those who are different from us with compassion, respect, and kindness.

Role of Christians in addressing diversity

The biblical call for an inclusive community without ethnic or national boundaries often challenges those in predominantly white Christian circles, especially individuals drawn to Christian nationalism in the United States. This call challenges us to repent of evil suspicions toward outgroups we've been culturally conditioned to view as threats. It requires the painful work of crucifying our prejudices to die with Christ so we can be resurrected into a new, redeemed humanity defined by love for all rather than fear of the other.

Admittedly, this is far easier said than done. Even in the most racially and ethnically diverse churches today, we struggle at times with tribalistic divisions, assumptions, and suspicions becoming codified in separate friend groups, side-taking, and miscommunication. All too often, we retreat into our comfortable cultural enclaves rather than mastering the Christ-like skill of treating every person as our equal, worthy of being embraced as a brother or sister in the family of God.

This is why the renewal of our minds through God's Word, shared life, and emulation of Jesus must become an ongoing discipline for us both individually and corporately. We must become students of our blind spots, question our assumptions, and stay humble. Always seek wisdom and accept corrections from fellow disciples who can point out biases and misconceptions influenced by our flawed world.

For individuals affected by oppression, the cautious and defensive behaviors developed for survival can gradually become ingrained biases, making reconciliation more challenging. The cycle of mistrust must find its resolution in truth, forgiveness, and the liberating power of God's Spirit. Otherwise, former victims simply become the latest version of oppressors, and the generational cycle continues.

For all involved, whether historically oppressed or privileged, the path forward into God's reconciled beloved community requires a supernatural openness and a surrender to Christ's ways. We must be willing to empty our evil suspicion of others and to be filled with the agape love that sees every human being through the eyes of the cross. The blood of Christ has torn down all.

Overcome scapegoating and build inclusive communities

To follow Christ's teachings means to actively foster inclusivity and respect in our communities. To truly reflect His love, Christians can take intentional steps to overcome scapegoating and embrace diversity, ensuring that every individual is valued and welcomed. Here are some practical ways to make this vision a reality:

- **Educate yourself and others.** Learn about different cultures, histories, and experiences to better understand and appreciate the diversity around us. Share this knowledge with others to promote empathy and reduce prejudice.
- **Build genuine relationships.** Take the time to get to know people who are different from you. Listen to their stories, share your own, and find common ground. Build genuine relationships to help break down barriers and foster mutual respect.
- **Speak out against injustice.** Use your voices to challenge harmful stereotypes, discrimination, and xenophobia. Advocate for policies and practices that promote equality and justice for all.
- **Practice hospitality.** Open your homes and hearts to those who are different from you. Show hospitality to strangers, just as Christ welcomed us into His family.

By following these principles, we can create a more inclusive and compassionate society that reflects the love and justice of God. Let us be the light that shines in the darkness, bringing hope and healing to a divided world.

The Biblical command against fear

Scapegoating invokes widespread fear—fear from the targeted people as well as fear from those who feel compassion for those who are targeted. Throughout the Bible, God commands His people not to fear. This command is rooted in the understanding that God is sovereign and in control of all circumstances. God tells Joshua, *"Have I not commanded you? Be strong and courageous. Do not be afraid; do not be discouraged, for the Lord your God will be with you wherever you go."* (Joshua 1:9).

In the New Testament, Jesus reiterates this command, saying, *"Peace I leave with you; my peace I give you. I do not give to you as the world gives. Do not let your hearts be troubled and do not be afraid."* (John 14:27). This peace is not dependent on external circumstances but is rooted in the presence and promises of God.

The role of faith in overcoming fear

Faith plays a crucial role in overcoming fear. Hebrews 11, often referred to as the "Faith Hall of Fame," highlights the stories of individuals who acted in faith despite their fears. From Noah building the ark to Abraham leaving his homeland, these examples show that faith involves trusting God even when circumstances are uncertain or frightening.

In the face of political fear, faith enables Christians to trust that God is in control and to act in ways that reflect His love and justice. It calls for a reliance on God's power and wisdom rather than human strength and understanding.

Historical examples of faith overcoming political fear

Throughout history, there have been numerous examples of Christians who faced political fear with unwavering faith. During the Roman Empire, early Christians were persecuted for their faith. Despite the threat of imprisonment, torture, and death, many remained steadfast. Their faith not only sustained them but also inspired others and contributed to the spread of Christianity.

During the Civil Rights Movement in the United States, many leaders were motivated by their Christian faith to stand against racial injustice. Figures like Martin Luther King Jr. drew strength from their belief in a just and loving God. King's famous "I Have a Dream" speech is deeply rooted in biblical imagery and the hope of God's kingdom on earth.

Theological reflections on courage and justice

Courage and justice are integral aspects of the Christian response to political fear. Theologically, courage is not the absence of fear but the willingness to act correctly despite the presence of fear. This is evident in the lives of biblical figures like Esther and Daniel. Esther risked her life to save her people even though they were targets of scapegoating by Haman. Daniel continued to pray despite the threat of being thrown into the lion's den.

Justice, on the other hand, is a core attribute of God's character. The Bible repeatedly calls God's people to pursue justice and defend the oppressed. We are told *"Learn to do right; seek justice. Defend the oppressed. Take up the cause of the fatherless; plead the case of the widow."* (Isaiah 1:17). This pursuit of justice often requires courage to stand against fear-driven policies and actions.

Practical guidelines for Christians facing political fear

Consider the following guidelines to overcome political fear:

- **Build a strong faith foundation.** Regularly engage with Scripture and prayer to strengthen your faith. This foundation will provide the resilience needed to face political fear.
- **Cultivate community.** Surround yourself with a supportive Christian community that can provide encouragement, accountability, and wisdom.
- **Advocate for righteousness.** Use your voice and influence to advocate for policies that align with biblical principles of justice and compassion. Be a witness to God's kingdom values in the public sphere.
- **Practice empathy.** Seek to understand the fears and concerns of others, even those with different political views. This empathy can bridge divides and foster constructive dialogue.
- **Rely on God's strength.** Acknowledge your limitations and rely on God's strength and guidance. Trust that He is working through you to accomplish His purposes.

Chapter 4: The impact of political fear on society

Fear has a profound effect on people, especially in the political realm. It drives such passionate feelings that it often overrides reason and forms strong bonds of identity. A podcaster once noted about televised wrestling that there are villains who are jeered and favorites who are cheered. Similarly, when a candidate, party, or group of people is seen as a villain, the masses can be whipped into a frenzy of hate. This collective identity, formed in opposition to the perceived villain, can lead to heinous crimes being committed by individuals who feel invisible within the crowd.

Fear is a powerful motivator in politics. When political fear makes us feel like our identity is under threat, fear becomes personal, emotional, and powerful. It can sway opinions, drive votes, and diminish voter turnout. Fear tactics are nearly twice as effective as messages without fear, as they tap into our instinct to find safety in numbers.[8] This strategy was used effectively by both Hitler and Stalin to consolidate power and control their populations.

This phenomenon was evident in Nazi Germany when Adolf Hitler took the stage to speak to rapturous crowds. Hitler's speeches captivated a Germany bent on world domination, and his rhetoric fueled a nationalistic fervor that led to the atrocities of World War II and the Holocaust.[9,10,11] The same can be said of Joseph Stalin, "The Man of Steel," who enforced his vision for a communist world with brutal efficiency. Stalin's reign was

---

[8] Waldroff, Kirk. "Fear: A Powerful Motivator in Elections." *American Psychological Association*, 13 Oct. 2020, https://www.apa.org/news/apa/2020/fear-motivator-elections.

[9] "Nazi Germany." *Americanhistory.si.edu*, https://americanhistory.si.edu/explore/exhibitions/price-of-freedom/online/world-war-ii/axis-aggression/nazi-germany. Accessed 10 Nov. 2024.

[10] Miller, Chris. "Deseret News Archives: World First Learns of Adolf Hitler from 1923 'Beer-Hall Putsch.'" *Deseret News (Salt Lake City, Utah: 1964)*, Deseret News, 8 Nov. 2024, https://www.deseret.com/utah/2024/11/08/deseret-news-archives-world-learns-of-adolf-hitler-from-1923-beer-hall-putsch/.

[11] Onion, Amanda. "Adolf Hiter: Rise to Power, Impact & Death." *HISTORY*, 29 Oct. 2009, https://www.history.com/topics/world-war-ii/adolf-hitler-1.

marked by widespread fear and repression as he sought to expand communism beyond the Soviet Union and secure his position in world affairs.[12],[13],[14]

The politics of fear is not limited to historical examples. It continues to be a dynamic vector in the constitution of social bonds, legitimizing social exclusions and animosities.[15] Understanding how fear is used in politics can help us resist its effects and strive for a more rational and compassionate society.

The wide reach of political fear

Political fear is wide-reaching, subjecting the Christian community to sociopolitical, psychological, and physiological divisions.

The psychological impact of political fear

Fear has significant psychological effects on individuals and communities. People who are constantly exposed to fear-inducing messages can have heightened anxiety, stress, and a sense of helplessness. This psychological state can impair critical thinking, making people more susceptible to manipulation and less likely to engage in constructive dialogue.

The physiological impact of political fear

Research has shown that fear can trigger the fight-or-flight response, a physiological reaction that prepares the body to confront or flee a threat. While this response can be beneficial in situations of immediate danger, prolonged exposure to fear can lead to chronic stress, which has detrimental

---

[12] https://www.jstor.org/stable/3143688

[13] "What Were Joseph Stalin's Goals as World War Two Ended." *Dailyhistory.org*, https://www.dailyhistory.org/What_were_Joseph_Stalin's_goals_as_World_War_Two_ended. Accessed 10 Nov. 2024.

[14] "Communism: Karl Marx to Joseph Stalin." *Unc.edu*, https://europe.unc.edu/iron-curtain/history/communism-karl-marx-to-joseph-stalin/. Accessed 10 Nov. 2024.

[15] Gonçalves, Lara Sartorio. "The politics of fear and the authoritarian political imagination." *Isa-sociology.org*, https://globaldialogue.isa-sociology.org/articles/the-politics-of-fear-and-the-authoritarian-political-imagination. Accessed 10 Nov. 2024.

effects on mental and physical health. Chronic stress can contribute to conditions such as depression, anxiety disorders, cardiovascular disease, and a weakened immune system.

The sociopolitical impact of political fear

Fear also has profound sociopolitical effects. It can create divisions within society as people become more suspicious and less trusting of those who are different from them. This division can lead to marginalization of certain groups and the erosion of social cohesion. In extreme cases, division can result in violence and conflict.

Fear-driven politics can undermine democratic processes. When used to influence public opinion and policy, fear can lead to the erosion of civil liberties and human rights. Governments may justify authoritarian measures and restrictions on freedom in the name of security, leading to a reduction in democratic accountability and transparency.

Examples of the impact of political fear on social unity

The following examples show how political fear can generate discrimination and social division:

- **The Red Scare in the United States.** During the early to mid-20th century, fear of communism led to widespread suspicion and the persecution of individuals perceived to be sympathetic to communist ideologies. **During the McCarthy era, civil liberties were violated through blacklisting, imprisonment, or ostracism on unproven accusations.**
- **Apartheid in South Africa.** The apartheid regime used fear of racial integration to justify the systemic oppression of the non-white population. Fear-mongering about the loss of cultural identity and economic stability was used to maintain the status quo of racial segregation and inequality.
- **The refugee crisis in Europe.** Fear of terrorism and economic instability has been used to justify restrictive immigration policies and the marginalization of refugees. This has led to a rise in xenophobia and discrimination, undermining the principles of compassion and solidarity.

Theological reflections on fear and community

Theologically, the Church is called to be a community of love, peace, and justice. The fear that divides and alienates is antithetical to the Gospel message. The early church in Acts 2:42-47 is a model of a community that lived out the principles of love and unity, sharing their resources and caring for one another's needs.

The concept of the "body of Christ" (1 Corinthians 12) underscores the interconnectedness of believers. Just as a body functions harmoniously when all parts work together, the Church is called to function as a unified body, overcoming fear and division through mutual care and support.

Scriptural insights on fear and division

The Bible provides guidance for overcoming fear and promoting unity.

In Ephesians 2:14-16, Paul speaks of Christ breaking down the "dividing wall of hostility" between different groups, creating one new humanity. He emphasizes the importance of reconciliation and unity in the body of Christ.

In 1 John 4:18, we read, *"There is no fear in love. But perfect love drives out fear because fear has to do with punishment. The one who fears is not made perfect in love."* This verse highlights the transformative power of love in overcoming fear and fostering unity.

In speaking directly against fear, we as human beings desperately need the assurance of the presence of God in our lives and His work on our behalf. His words, *"I will be with you,"* provide the source and only hope for our relief. While Israel was in captivity in Babylon, the LORD spoke of His comforting presence through the prophet Isaiah.

Consider the following powerful messages of assurance and divine support:

"So do not fear, for I am with you; do not be dismayed, for I am your God. I will strengthen you and help you; I will uphold you with my righteous right hand." (Isaiah 41:10).

This verse addresses the fears and anxieties of the Israelites. God reassures them that they need not fear or be dismayed because He is with them. The reference to God's "righteous right hand" symbolizes His power and justice, indicating His ability to provide strength and support.

"For I am the LORD, your God, who takes hold of your right hand and says to you, Do not fear; I will help you." (Isaiah 41:13).

Here, God emphasizes His role as a personal deity who is intimately involved in the lives of His people. The imagery of God taking hold of their right hand signifies His guidance and protection, further reinforcing the message of not fearing because He will provide help.

The combined message of these verses is one of profound encouragement and divine faithfulness. Let's expound on each element:

Do not fear, for I am with you.

Fear is a natural response to uncertainty and threat, but God's presence is a powerful antidote. This assurance is intended to calm the hearts of the Israelites, reminding them that they are not alone in their struggles.

Do not be dismayed, for I am your God.

Dismay often comes from feeling abandoned or powerless. By asserting "I am your God," the Lord reaffirms His covenant relationship with His people, a bond that carries promises of protection and care.

I will strengthen you and help you.

These words promise divine empowerment. In times of weakness or challenge, God provides the necessary strength and assistance, ensuring His people can endure and overcome their difficulties.

I will uphold you with my righteous right hand.

This is a pledge of God's unwavering support and justice. His "righteous right hand" signifies His authority and commitment to uphold His people through righteous actions.

I am the LORD, your God, who takes hold of your right hand.

The personal nature of this statement underscores God's intimate involvement in the lives of the Israelites. It portrays a God who is not distant but actively engaged, guiding and protecting them.

Do not fear; I will help you.

The repetition of the command to not fear, coupled with the promise of help, underscores the reliability and certainty of God's intervention. It is a call to trust in His providence and sovereign will.

Historical context of early Christian persecution

The early Christians faced severe persecution under the Roman Empire, beginning with Emperor Nero's reign in AD 64.[16] Nero blamed Christians for the Great Fire of Rome and subjected them to brutal tortures and executions. This marked the beginning of a series of persecutions that continued intermittently until the Edict of Milan in AD 313, which granted religious tolerance throughout the empire.[17]

Examples of fearlessness in early Christians

Early Christian martyrs exemplify the fearless spirit that Christians are encouraged to embody today. Their unwavering faith and courage in the face of persecution serve as a timeless reminder of the transformative power of martyrdom and the enduring strength of the Christian faith.

- **Stephen, the first martyr.** Stephen, one of the first deacons of the Christian Church, was stoned to death by the Jewish Council for his faith. His martyrdom is recorded in Acts 7:54-60 and serves as an example of unwavering faith and courage in the face of death.
- **Perpetua and Felicity.** Perpetua, a young noblewoman, and Felicity, a pregnant slave, were martyred in Carthage in AD 203. Despite the threat of death, they remained steadfast in their faith and faced their execution with remarkable bravery.[18]

---

[16] Uggerud, Kristoffer. "The Early Christian Martyrs: Persecutions in the Roman Empire." *The Collector*, 10 June 2023, https://www.thecollector.com/early-christian-martyrs/.

[17] "The Edict of Milan - Lactantius." *Earlychurchtexts.com*, https://earlychurchtexts.com/public/edict_of_milan.htm. Accessed 11 Nov. 2024.

[18] Uggerud, Kristoffer. "The Early Christian Martyrs: Persecutions in the Roman Empire." *The Collector*, 10 June 2023, https://www.thecollector.com/early-christian-martyrs/.

- **Ignatius of Antioch.** Ignatius, the Bishop of Antioch, was condemned to be devoured by wild beasts in the Roman Colosseum. On his way to Rome, he wrote letters encouraging Christians to remain faithful and not fear death.[19]
- **Tertullian.** Tertullian, a prolific early Christian author and apologist, famously stated, *"The blood of the martyrs is the seed of the Church."* This powerful quote encapsulates the transformative power of martyrdom within the Christian faith. Although Christians were targeted politically, they lived in such a sacrificial serving manner that the Church grew and had an impact on society. The quote suggests that sacrifices and sufferings of martyrs serve as a catalyst for the growth and expansion of the Church.[20]

The fearlessness exhibited by early Christians serves as a powerful example for contemporary believers. Tertullian's quote reminds us that the sacrifices of martyrs have historically led to the growth and strengthening of the Church. This legacy of courage and faith can inspire modern Christians to stand firm in their beliefs, even in the face of adversity.

Overcome divisiveness and build a fearless community

The following guidelines can help to build a fearless community:

- **Foster inclusive dialogue.** Create spaces for open and respectful conversations where diverse perspectives are valued. This can help build understanding and reduce fear of the unknown.
- **Promote compassion and empathy.** Encourage acts of kindness and compassion towards those who are different or marginalized. This can help break down barriers and build trust.
- **Educate on fear tactics.** Raise awareness about the ways fear is used in political discourse. Educating others can empower them to recognize and resist manipulation.

---

[19] Ibid

[20] "Tertullian: 'The Blood of the Martyrs Is the Seed of the Church.'" *The Socratic Method*, 8 Nov. 2023, https://www.socratic-method.com/quote-meanings/tertullian-the-blood-of-the-martyrs-is-the-seed-of-the-church.

- **Advocate for justice.** Stand against policies and actions that marginalize or harm vulnerable groups. Advocate for justice, equality, and human dignity.
- **Strengthen community bonds.** Invest in building strong, supportive communities where people feel valued and connected. This can create a sense of security and belonging that counters fear.

Chapter 5: Christian nationalism: When faith becomes political power

Throughout history, the pursuit of power has led many astray, especially when it's cloaked in religious rhetoric. Christian nationalism is one of the clearest examples of this. It presents itself as a movement to restore morality and create a society built on a specific interpretation of Christianity. But beneath its promises lies a more troubling truth: the worship of power itself.

When faith is used as a tool to control, exclude, or dominate others, it moves away from its true purpose—leading people toward love, justice, and humility. Instead of serving God, Christian nationalism often serves political ambitions, shaping beliefs to fit an agenda rather than the teachings of Christ.

True faith should inspire compassion, not division. It should bring people together in understanding, not separate them by ideology. When Christianity is twisted to justify political control, it no longer reflects Christ's message of grace and unity. Instead, it becomes an idol of power, demanding loyalty and devotion at the expense of true faith.

History and the rebirth of Christian nationalism

History is replete with examples of this dangerous conflation of faith and power. Consider the Crusades, ostensibly religious wars undertaken in the name of Christianity that resulted in immense suffering and bloodshed. While the motives of the participants were undoubtedly complex and varied, the use of religious fervor to justify military conquest and territorial expansion exemplifies a profound distortion of Christian values.

Similarly, the Spanish Inquisition, with its brutal methods of enforcing religious conformity, stands as a stark reminder of the horrors that can result when religious zeal is combined with unchecked political power. Even seemingly more benign instances of the Church aligning itself with state power throughout history frequently led to the suppression of dissent, the persecution of minority groups, and the perpetuation of social inequalities.

The contemporary resurgence of Christian nationalism is deeply intertwined with the rise of populist movements across the globe. These movements often rally their base by appealing to a sense of national identity; cultural preservation; and concerns about immigration, globalization, and perceived threats. The rhetoric frequently demonizes those perceived as "outsiders," constructing an us-versus-them mentality that can have dire consequences.

Furthermore, the digital age has amplified this phenomenon. The internet and social media provide fertile ground for the dissemination of misinformation and the creation of echo chambers, where like-minded individuals reinforce each other's biases, creating an environment where critical thinking is stifled. The rapid spread of disinformation makes it difficult to counter these narratives effectively, further strengthening the grip of those who promote Christian nationalism.

The appeal of Christian nationalism

The seductive whisper of power, particularly when draped in the mantle of religious righteousness, is a siren song that has lured countless individuals and institutions astray throughout history. Christian nationalism, in its various guises, represents a particularly insidious manifestation of this temptation. It promises a restoration of societal order, a return to perceived moral foundations, and the establishment of a nation reflecting a specifically interpreted Christian worldview. But this promise, alluring as it may seem, often masks a deeper, more dangerous reality: the idolatry of power itself.

The appeal of Christian nationalism often lies in its promise of security and stability in an increasingly uncertain world. Fear, a potent motivator in human affairs, is frequently exploited by those who seek to consolidate power.

Christian nationalists present a simplified narrative, portraying a world beset by enemies both internal and external, and offering themselves as the solution. Their narrative often casts those who hold different beliefs or belong to different groups as threats, fostering an atmosphere of suspicion and animosity. Instead of fostering unity and understanding, they generate division and resentment. They create fertile ground for the rise of authoritarian tendencies, causing individuals to relinquish their critical thinking abilities in exchange for a perceived sense of security offered by a strong leader or ideology.

The use of inflammatory rhetoric and conspiracy theories further fuels this narrative. By disseminating misinformation and exploiting existing anxieties, proponents of Christian nationalism can cultivate a sense of urgency and fear, thereby mobilizing support for their agenda. This dangerous game can easily lead to the demonization of entire groups of people, justifying acts of violence and discrimination.

The distortion of Christian teachings is often central to this strategy. The Bible is selectively interpreted to support pre-existing political agendas, with verses taken out of context or twisted to fit a particular narrative. The emphasis is frequently placed on the commands to obey authorities, while ignoring equally important injunctions to love one's neighbor and to seek justice for the oppressed. This selective interpretation is a form of religious manipulation, using faith as a tool to gain and maintain power.

The problem with Christian nationalism

The core problem isn't necessarily the desire to see Christian values reflected in public life; many Christians throughout history have actively sought to improve society through their faith. The crucial distinction lies in the *means* employed and the *ends* pursued.

Authentic Christian engagement in the political sphere is characterized by humility, a commitment to justice for all, and a recognition of the inherent dignity of every human being, regardless of their beliefs. It is grounded in the radical love exemplified by Jesus Christ, who prioritized the marginalized and challenged the powerful. He embraced the cross, the ultimate symbol of self-sacrifice, rather than seeking political power.

Christian nationalism, however, often inverts this paradigm. It frequently adopts a posture of dominance, seeking to impose its beliefs upon others through legislative and social pressure, rather than persuading them through love and reason. This approach betrays a fundamental misunderstanding of the nature of the Kingdom of God, which is not a terrestrial empire to be established through force, but a spiritual reality that transcends national boundaries and political structures. The Kingdom of God is not defined by political power, but by love, justice, mercy, and compassion.

The danger of Christian nationalism

White supremacist groups have distorted Christian teachings to justify race-based hatred, misusing Christ's name to validate their exclusionary beliefs. Their ideology elevates racial supremacy to the level of devotion, making it an idol—something revered above the true message of Christ. In Scripture, an idol is anything that takes the place of God in one's heart, commanding allegiance that rightfully belongs to Him alone.

Through ethnic prejudice and hatred, Christian nationalists usurp Christ and replace Him, rendering any supposed Christian identity they claim as baseless. They reveal the dark insecurities behind such racism and xenophobia within segments of modern American society, particularly among many white supremacists who propagate hatred against immigrants and people of color under the false banners of "Christianity" and "the good people of our nation."

The tragic fact is that any belief system or philosophy based on hating, harming, or seeking to erase any person or group made in the image of God, stands in defiance of the life and teachings of Jesus Christ.

In essence, the words reveal how any nationalistic prejudices based purely in ethnic/racial identities are rooted fundamentally in a fear—literally "a frantic fear of poverty" and a false belief of "scarcity." There is a fear that immigrants or minority populations are seeking to take what isn't theirs, using up or depleting finite resources. And often attached to that fear are suspicions around security, safety, and what future will be left for one's own children and grandchildren.

Truly, these issues stem from a poverty of spirit—the inability to see all people as human, loved by God, and created in His image. It is shortsighted to love only your own and hate others. But this is how racism and hatred works. It reduces human beings made in the image of God to soulless objects and "types." It diminishes their humanity by refusing to see them as people at all.

The antidote for Christian nationalism

The antidote for this dangerous trend lies not in withdrawing from the public square, but in engaging with it in a thoughtful, informed, and ethically responsible way. Christians have a vital role to play in advocating for justice, promoting peace, and working towards a more equitable society. This role requires a willingness to engage in critical self-reflection, to challenge our own biases, and to enter into respectful dialogue with those who hold differing views. It requires a commitment to truth-seeking and a willingness to confront injustice wherever it may be found, even when it's uncomfortable or challenging. It also involves a commitment to theological literacy and critical engagement with religious rhetoric. Christians must be able to discern between genuine expressions of faith and distorted interpretations used to justify political power grabs.

The task before the Church is a momentous call to reject the idolatrous worship of power and return to the fundamental principles of the Christian faith—love, justice, mercy, and humility. It is a call to resist the seductive allure of nationalistic fervor and to embrace a vision of the Kingdom of God that transcends national borders and political ideologies. Only by reclaiming the authentic message of the Gospel can we hope to build a society that reflects the love and compassion of Jesus Christ.

The path forward involves a commitment to dialogue, truth-telling, and a steadfast devotion to justice for all, regardless of background or beliefs. Only then can we truly separate faith from the politics of power and create a world where love prevails, not dominance. The struggle for this true faith is a constant one, requiring vigilance, humility, and unwavering dedication to the principles of the Gospel. The stakes are high, and the consequences of inaction are far-reaching.

Theological views on fear, courage, and action

Theologically, courage is a virtue that enables believers to act in accordance with their faith, even in the face of fear. This courage is not about the absence of fear but about trusting in God's power and presence. In Joshua 1:9, God commands Joshua to be strong and courageous, reminding him that the Lord is with him wherever he goes.

49

In the New Testament, the early Christians exemplified this courage. Despite persecution and martyrdom, they boldly proclaimed the Gospel and lived out their faith. Their courage was rooted in their hope in the resurrection and their trust in God's ultimate victory.

Personal stories of overcoming political fear

Consider the following personal stories of individuals who overcame political fear through resistance:

- **Corrie ten Boom.** During World War II, Corrie ten Boom and her family helped hide Jews from the Nazis. Despite the constant threat of discovery and death, her faith in God gave her the courage to continue her work. Her story is a testament to the power of faith in overcoming fear.

- **Dietrich Bonhoeffer.** A German pastor and theologian, Bonhoeffer actively opposed the Nazi regime and was involved in plots to assassinate Hitler. His deep faith and theological convictions gave him the strength to resist fear and stand for justice, even at the cost of his life.

- **Rosa Parks.** Known as the mother of the civil rights movement, Rosa Parks' refusal to give up her bus seat was an act of defiance against racial segregation. Her faith and commitment to justice fueled her courage to stand against fear and oppression.

Guidelines for overcoming fear

Follow these strategies for overcoming fear:

- **Ground yourself in Scripture.** Regularly read and meditate on Bible passages that speak to fear and faith. Let God's word guide and strengthen you.

- **Cultivate a prayerful life.** Develop a habit of prayer, bringing your fears and concerns to God. Trust in His wisdom and guidance.

- **Get community support.** Surround yourself with a supportive community of faith. Share your fears and seek encouragement and accountability.

- **Engage in acts of service.** Channel your fears into positive actions that serve others and promote justice. Serving others can help shift your focus from fear to compassion.
- **Stay informed and critical.** Educate yourself about political issues and critically evaluate the information you receive. Seek out diverse perspectives and avoid fear-mongering sources.

Guidelines for personal courage and advocacy

When faced with political fear, consider the following guidelines for personal courage:

- **Identify your fears.** Reflect on your personal fears related to politics. Write them down and pray for God's help in overcoming them.
- **Take small steps.** Start with small acts of courage and advocacy. This can help build your confidence and resilience over time.
- **Partner with others.** Find like-minded individuals or groups to join in your advocacy efforts. Working together can amplify your impact and provide mutual support.
- **Use your gifts.** Identify your unique gifts and talents and find ways to use them in addressing political fear and promoting justice.
- **Reflect and adjust.** Regularly reflect on your actions and their impact. Be willing to adjust your approach as needed and seek God's guidance continually.

Chapter 6: Christian nationalism: Dangers of idolatry

An idol, by definition, is something other than God that becomes an object of profound admiration or devotion—something that takes the place of God in our hearts and lives. Throughout human history, various peoples and cultures have embraced certain idols, whether physical objects, ideas, or philosophies that took precedence over the one true God. The Bible warns repeatedly against idolatry, as it leads people astray into false worship and away from the reverence and devotion that is due to the Creator alone.

One manifestation of modern idolatry has been the phenomenon of Christian nationalism, which has taken insidious root in various nations and cultures around the world. At its core, Christian nationalism is the blending of one's national and cultural identity with a perverse, distorted view of Christianity. It's a dangerous path, as it risks turning the nation into an idol. Patriotism can become a form of idolatry where the nation is worshipped more than the Creator. We can see this dynamic clearly in the words,

> *"Has a nation changed its gods, even though they are not gods? But my people have exchanged their glorious God for worthless idols... They have forsaken me, the spring of living water, and have dug their own cisterns, broken cisterns that cannot hold water."* (Jeremiah 2:11-13).

About Christian nationalism and idolatry

It's important for followers of Jesus Christ to clearly express in words and actions the life and teachings of Jesus in such a way that others would not be confused about our intentions when dealing with different ethnicities. In fact, Christ teaches this when He issues the Great Commission, *"Go, make disciples of all the nations."* (Matthew 28:20).

Some people have associated the Christian faith, as taught by Jesus Christ, with a form of Christianity (known as Christian nationalism) that emphasizes patriotism. For example, some political groups today use Christian symbols and language to promote policies that are exclusionary or discriminatory. This association can create a false equivalence between true Christian teachings and a nationalistic agenda, leading to misunderstandings about the nature of Christianity.

About patriotism to nations

As generations came and went, deeply rooted beliefs about our nation have been passed along. The love of our parents and the land of our fathers is "patriotism." In a sense, it is right to love and honor the land in which we live. In Genesis 12:1-4, we read a promise to Abraham that all "nations" would be blessed through him. That blessing comes through Jesus Christ.

Acts 17:26 indicates that God placed each person in a land and a nation. Later in Revelations 7, we see that there will be people from every "tribe, language, and nation" who will render worship to the Lamb of God (Jesus Christ) eternally. So clearly "nations" are a part of the plan of God.

But what happens when people exalt "nations" to a "god" and "idol? Babylon! Egypt! The Pax Romana! The Heavenly mandate of the Mongolian empire! The Third Reich of Germany! The Belgian Congo!

How patriotism morphs into Christian nationalism

For the Christian nationalist, the nation itself becomes an idol to be worshipped. Patriotism mutates into a twisted road where the love of country is raised above love for God. In America, instead of embracing that we are "one nation under God," some Christian nationalists act as though we are "one God under nation."

The nation is viewed as the source for blessings instead of as the recipient. As when the ancient Israelites pursued earthly wealth without God, it was likened to digging a well or a cistern with cracks in it that could not hold water. Patriotism mutates into a twisted road where people place the love of country above the love for God. And inevitably, it will not fully satisfy like the true "Living Water" of God Himself.

In the Apostle Paul's letter to the Roman church, he taught that man has sinned against God and incurred His wrath. An aspect of that sin is the making of idols rather than worshipping the Living God. Included in idol making is a rejection of God's revelation and instead embracing man-made images of animals and people. In his letter, Paul writes:

"For since the creation of the world God's invisible qualities—his eternal power and divine nature—have been clearly seen, being understood from what has been made, so that people are without excuse. For although they knew God, they neither glorified him as God nor gave thanks to him, but their thinking became futile and their foolish hearts were darkened. Although they claimed to be wise, they became fools and exchanged the glory of the immortal God for images made to look like a mortal human being and birds and animals and reptiles." (Romans 1:20-23).

Later in this same book, Paul declares that *"All have sinned, and fall short of the glory of God."* (Romans 3:23). Every people group globally worships idols. Indeed, Christian nationalism manifests wherever people, often out of arrogance and pride, craft their cultural and ethnic identity onto the cross of Christ to create a revolting hybrid of the holy and the profane.

The historical context of the Ku Klux Klan's principles shows how Christian nationalism can distort religious teachings for political and social control. This distortion is not limited to the past. Modern movements continue to blend religious rhetoric with nationalistic goals, leading to confusion and division.

On January 6th, 2021, Christian nationalists bearing their particular phrase called out could be heard chanting "You will not replace us!" as they assaulted the U.S. Capitol.

Some Christian nationalists have adopted mottos like "Deutschland uber alles" or "Turkey for the Turks!" Or "Croatia for Croats" or the phrase called out, "Go back to \-\-\--." Each expression combines devotion to nation and race with cultural domination and violence toward the perceived enemies of the nation.

Nationalism and idolatry throughout the ages

This section highlights some examples of this nationalism and idolatry throughout the ages.

Old Testament examples

The Scriptures state that as the Jewish population grew in ancient Egypt, they became a target of suspicion. Rulers believed that as the numbers increased, the Jews might switch allegiances and pose a threat to them.

Based on that suspicion the Egyptians went about the task of enslaving the Jews. The enslavement included setting taskmasters over them and instituting a form of oppression that would affect them and their families systematically for generations. All these events took place until God rescued them through Moses, bringing them freedom from Egypt.

New Testament examples

The New Testament church consisted of a mixture of ethnic groups, Jews and gentiles alike. Some people were freeborn, some enslaved, some in bondage, and others were in the possession of the enslaved at some time.

The Pharisees combined their Jewish heritage with pride over their ethnic credentials, asking "Are you calling us Samaritans and possessed by demons?" In other words, God's chosen people saw themselves culturally superior to the half-breed Samaritans because, "We are true Jews, not dogs!" When the Gospel spread in Acts, Christian Jews began accepting converts from other peoples. But soon radical Jewish Christians cried "Keep your vile creed away from us - you Gentile swine!"

The Apostle Paul gave instructions about how diverse groups were to relate to each other, even for those experiencing enslavement. Note that enslavement was different from the more recent form of chattel slavery in America, as they were to live noble lives even during the most challenging times. Paul's instructions warned against a certain kind of person who practiced evil suspicions and conversations that were of no help to others.

Historic examples

The American experience shows that, Indigenous people lived in the Americas with their languages, cultures, and customs, and they owned these lands for ages. As explorers traveled the world, contact with Portuguese and Spanish conquistadors during the 15th and 16th centuries led to the conquering of America and the decimation of tribes by war and largely by disease. These conquests were endorsed by Papal announcements as early as 1492 from Pope Alexander the VI declaring,

> *"And we make, appoint, and depute you and your said heirs and successors lords of them with full and free power, authority, and jurisdiction of every kind…"* —Pope Alexander VI, "Inter Caetera" [21]

Some people also traveled to the Americas peacefully, fleeing religious persecution to live a pilgrim life in America. In the 17th and 18th centuries, the Dutch, French, and British joined the Portuguese and Spanish in the transatlantic slave trade. Over time, each nation devised its classifications of citizens versus foreigners and what was of vital interest to their nation. The Spanish used *Sistema de Castas* (1531-1800), a racial classification system, to create their "society of castes" which was used to order how the races were to live, with varying degrees of freedom. **Spanish colonial laws in the New World institutionalized systems of control over the conquered territories of the Maya, Aztec, and other indigenous populations.** [22]

The Knights of the Ku Klux Klan (KKK), as now organized, is a patriotic, benevolent, fraternal order. To be eligible for membership in this all-American order, one must have been born in the United States, of white parentage, be over eighteen years of age, and of the Protestant Christian faith.[23]

Many people would be shocked if they read the Principles and Purposes of the Knights of the Ku Klux Klan outside of the context of their history and terrorizing legacy against Black people, Jews, Immigrants, and Catholics. The KKK holds the following chief aims:

---

[21]VI, Pope Alexander. "The Doctrine of Discovery, 1493." Gilderlehrman.org, 2012, https://www.gilderlehrman.org/sites/default/files/inline-pdfs/04093_FPS.pdf.

[22]B. Escobar Zelaya, Susana. "The Remains of Castas in Latin America." Global Insight: A Journal of Critical Human Science and Culture, vol. 2, no. 1, 2021, pp. 12–19, doi:10.32855/globalinsight.2021.002.

[23] "Principles and Purposes of the Knights of the Ku Klux Klan Are Outlined by an Exalted Cyclops of the Order." *Yale.edu*, https://collections.library.yale.edu/catalog/16173379?child_oid=16173608. Accessed 5 Sept. 2024.

- To preserve the Unites States as a Protestant Christian nation, bringing the different branches into a closer relationship with one another.
- To indoctrinate purer patriotism in its members.
- To uphold the Constitution and laws of the United States and the separate states thereof.
- To maintain, achieve, and perpetuate the free public schools.

This information, published in 1915 and distributed for decades, reflects a fusion of Christian teachings with a nationalistic agenda, forming a strange brew of false doctrine enforced by the threat of violence and the complicity of clergy and elected officials.

The following image shows an early KKK propaganda poster:

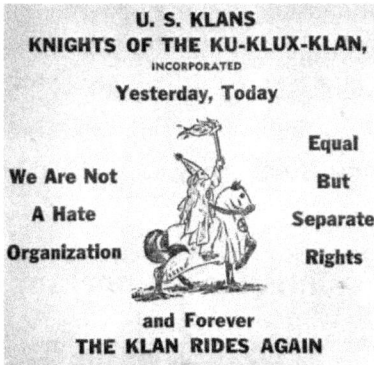

Modern-day examples

Politics can bring out the best and worst in people. During the events of January 6, 2021, we saw on display a protest that turned murderous. Some argue that Black Lives Matter (BLM) protests and George Floyd protesters were just as bad with violent outbreaks, destroyed properties, and people killed. Sin is Sin! Killing, violent protests, as well as acts of vandalism and looting is wrong when perpetrated by anyone—Democrat, Republican, Independent, or other. I am not writing to commend violence or even pacifism for the sake of peace (Romans 13). What's most concerning about the events on January 6th, 2021, is how the actions were ascribed to and dedicated to Jesus Christ.

Some individuals who were skeptical of the government became convinced by the deep state theory, thinking it was either staged or a hoax. Crosses were carried, T-shirts were emblazoned, and flags were waved in the name of Jesus Christ. Those who watched the world on most news stations witnessed a violent attempted coup on the nation's Capital that culminated with a moment of prayer in the halls of Congress. Thinking critically about the actual events, loss of lives, police officers beaten, and worst of all it is ascribed and dedicated to JESUS. January 6th, 2021, was truly a sad day.

The questions follow: Why invoke Jesus Christ? Does the Bible condone violent revolt? Does the American experience require violence to bring a change in society? Does the Kingdom of Heaven need me as an American citizen to take up arms? Could this apply in crime-ridden areas of my city? Or can violence be applied where corporate greed is present or local business owners with a history of injustice or immorality? Should we storm the local bar, club, or DMV? Who gets to judge? How are people saved? Born again? Should pastors lead the way with a heart to "die for America" because of their intense zeal for the United States? Or is there a better way? So many questions can arise from trying to understand the events of January 6th, 2021.

Comparison of Christianity and Christian nationalism

Although Christianity and Christian nationalism are sometimes intertwined, they differ significantly in their origins, focus, and objectives.

Christianity is a faith based on the teachings of Jesus Christ, emphasizing love, compassion, and the salvation of all people. It is inclusive, welcoming individuals from all backgrounds and ethnicities. The core message of Christianity is found in the Great Commandment, *"Love the Lord your God with all your heart and with all your soul and with all your mind" and "Love your neighbor as yourself."* (Matthew 22:37-39).

Christian nationalism, on the other hand, is a political ideology that merges Christian and nationalistic beliefs, often promoting the idea that the nation should be defined by its adherence to a particular interpretation of Christianity. This ideology can lead to exclusionary practices and policies, favoring one religious group over others and marginalizing those who don't fit the nationalistic criteria.

It's crucial for followers of Jesus Christ to differentiate between genuine Christian faith and Christian nationalism. This section compares the principals of Christianity with Christian nationalism.

Inclusivity vs. exclusivity

- **Christianity**. Jesus' teachings emphasize inclusivity. For example, in the Parable of the Good Samaritan (Luke 10:25-37), Jesus illustrates that love and compassion should extend beyond ethnic and religious boundaries.
- **Christian nationalism**. Promotes exclusivity, suggesting that only certain groups, such as White Protestants, are true members of the nation. This can lead to discrimination against minorities and non-Christians.

Focus on spiritual kingdom vs. earthly kingdom

- **Christianity**. Jesus taught that His kingdom is not of this world (John 18:36). The focus is on spiritual growth and preparing for eternal life.
- **Christian nationalism**. Emphasizes the importance of creating a nation that reflects their skewed interpretation of Christian values, often through political means and sometimes at the expense of others' rights.

Love and compassion vs. power and control

- **Christianity**. Central to Jesus' message is love and compassion for all people, including enemies (Matthew 5:44).
- **Christian nationalism**. Can prioritize power and control using religion to justify political and social dominance.

Separation of church and state

- **Christianity**. While Christians are encouraged to be good citizens, there is a recognition of the separation between church and state (Romans 13:1-7).
- **Christian nationalism**. Often seeks to blur or eliminate this separation, advocating for laws and policies that reflect their own religious beliefs.

Choose Christianity over Christian nationalism

By clearly expressing the life and teachings of Jesus, Christians can ensure that their actions reflect the inclusive, loving, and compassionate nature of their faith. This clarity is essential in a world where religious beliefs are often co-opted for political purposes, leading to division and misunderstanding.

Counteracting the influence of Christian nationalism necessitates a comprehensive strategy that highlights the core principles of Jesus Christ and encourages inclusivity, empathy, and compassion. Christians can adopt the following strategies to help accomplish these goals.

Endorse education and awareness

- **Study the Bible**. Deepen your understanding of the Bible and the teachings of Jesus. Focus on passages such as the Sermon on the Mount (Matthew 5-7) and the Parable of the Good Samaritan (Luke 10:25-37) that emphasize love, compassion, and inclusiveness.
- **Educate others**. Share your knowledge with others in your community. Organize Bible study groups, workshops, and seminars that focus on the differences between true Christian teachings and the distorted views of Christian nationalism.

Promote inclusivity

- **Embrace diversity**. Actively welcome and include people from diverse backgrounds, ethnicities, and beliefs in your church and community activities. This demonstrates the inclusive nature of Christianity.
- **Engage in interfaith dialogue**. Talk with people of other faiths to promote mutual understanding and respect. These conversations can help break down barriers and counteract the exclusivity promoted by Christian nationalism.

Live out Christian values

- **Practice love and compassion**. Show love and compassion in your daily interactions. Volunteer for community service projects, support social justice initiatives, and help those in need, regardless of their background.

- **Model Christ-like behavior.** Be a living example of Jesus' teachings, reflecting the values of humility, kindness, and selflessness.

Speak out against injustice

- **Condemn hate and violence.** Publicly denounce any form of hate, violence, or discrimination that is justified in the name of Christianity. Promote peace and justice through clear and respectful communication.
- **Support victims.** Stand with those who are marginalized or oppressed. Offer support and solidarity to communities affected by the actions of Christian nationalists.

Engage in political advocacy

- **Promote separation of church and state.** Encourage policies that maintain the separation of church and state. This helps ensure that religious beliefs are not used to justify discriminatory laws or practices.
- **Vote for inclusive leaders.** Support political candidates who promote inclusivity, equality, and justice for all people, regardless of their religious beliefs.

Foster community and unity

- **Build bridges.** Create opportunities for dialogue and collaboration between different groups within your community. This can help foster a sense of unity and shared purpose.
- **Celebrate differences.** Recognize and celebrate the diversity within your community. Host events that highlight different cultures, traditions, and perspectives.

Practice prayer and reflection

- **Seek guidance.** Pray for wisdom and guidance to address the challenges posed by Christian nationalism. Reflect on how you can be a positive influence in your community.

- **Encourage others**. Encourage fellow Christians to join you in these efforts. A collective approach can have a more significant impact.

By adopting these strategies, Christians can help counteract the distortion caused by Christian nationalism and promote a more authentic and inclusive expression of their faith.

Chapter 7: The role of Christians in addressing political fear

The Christian community plays a vital role in helping individuals overcome anxiety and fear. Through fellowship, believers can support and uplift each other, sharing burdens and encouraging one another in faith. The early church exemplified this communal support as seen in Acts 2:42-47, where believers shared everything they had and devoted themselves to teaching, fellowship, breaking bread, and prayer.

In modern times, small groups, prayer meetings, and church services continue to provide spaces for believers to connect, share their struggles, and find encouragement. By fostering a sense of belonging and mutual care, the Church can help individuals feel less isolated in their anxieties.

Challenges in addressing political fear

The early Christian Church emerged in a time of significant political turmoil and fear. The Roman Empire, with its vast power and influence, was a formidable force. The emperors demanded absolute loyalty and worship, often leading to severe persecution of those who refused to comply. Christians, with their unwavering allegiance to Christ, were seen as a threat to the stability and unity of the empire. Historical records, such as the works of Tacitus and Suetonius, provide vivid descriptions of the atrocities committed against Christians. These accounts highlight the intense fear and oppression that early Christians faced. Despite this, the Church grew and thrived, demonstrating the power of faith and resilience in the face of adversity.

In contemporary times, the Church continues to face various forms of political and social challenges. Issues such as religious persecution, political polarization, and social injustice are prevalent in many parts of the world. The politics of fear, characterized by divisive rhetoric and actions, continues to be a significant challenge for the Church.

Historic challenges and the politics of fear

The Christian Church has a profound history of overcoming persecution and growing stronger in the face of adversity. From its inception under the Roman Empire, the Church faced significant political and social challenges. Yet, the writings of the Apostles reflect a perspective that embraced suffering for a higher purpose, rooted in faith and resilience.

One of the most compelling examples is seen with the Apostle Peter who, despite denying Jesus Christ, was forgiven and became a pivotal leader in the early church. In his letter to the Church in Rome, Peter wrote powerful words that continue to inspire Christians facing trials:

"Blessed be the God and Father of our Lord Jesus Christ, who according to His great mercy has caused us to be born again to a living hope through the resurrection of Jesus Christ from the dead, to obtain an inheritance which is imperishable, undefiled, and will not fade away, reserved in heaven for you, who are protected by the power of God through faith for a salvation ready to be revealed in the last time. In this, you greatly rejoice, even though now for a little while, if necessary, you have been distressed by various trials, so that the proof of your faith, being more precious than gold which perishes though tested by fire, may be found to result in praise, glory, and honor at the revelation of Jesus Christ; and though you have not seen Him, you love Him, and though you do not see Him now, but believe in Him, you greatly rejoice with joy inexpressible and full of glory, obtaining as the outcome of your faith, the salvation of your souls." (1 Peter 1:3–9).

Peter's call for worship and trust in God, despite trials, emphasized the enduring value of faith, more precious than gold. This message was particularly profound under the brutal reign of the Roman Caesars, where Christians faced unimaginable persecution. Historical accounts, such as those by Suetonius in "The Twelve Caesars," describe the extreme cruelty faced by early Christians, including crucifixion, being set on fire, and being thrown into arenas with gladiators and wild animals.

Despite these trials, the early church thrived by embracing their faith and proclaiming, "Jesus is Lord" (Yesu Kurios) instead of "Caesar is Lord" (Kaiser Kurios), even under the threat of death. This defiance in the face of political fear highlighted their unwavering faith. The resilience of the early church provides valuable lessons for addressing the politics of fear in contemporary times. It demonstrates the power of faith, community, and the unwavering commitment to a higher purpose, even when faced with oppression and adversity.

Modern-day challenges and the politics of fear

In today's world, the Church continues to confront various forms of fear, whether political, social, or economic. The lessons from the early church can serve as a beacon of hope and a reminder of the importance of standing firm in one's faith and values.

The principles and teachings of the early church remain relevant. The emphasis on faith, community, and resilience can guide the modern Church in addressing these challenges. By drawing on the rich legacy of the early church, contemporary Christians can find strength and inspiration to navigate the complexities of today's world.

The Christian Church has a rich legacy of overcoming persecution and growing stronger in the face of adversity. The writings of the Apostles and the actions of early Christians provide valuable lessons for addressing the politics of fear. By remaining steadfast in faith, promoting unity and inclusivity, and actively engaging in social justice, the modern Church can continue to be a beacon of hope and resilience in a world often characterized by fear and division.

Through these efforts, the Church can continue to fulfill its mission of spreading the Gospel, serving those in need, and standing up for justice and righteousness. The legacy of the early church serves as a powerful reminder of the transformative power of faith and the importance of remaining true to one's values, even in the face of adversity.

The role of individual Christians in addressing fear

The writings of the Apostles, particularly Peter and Paul, emphasize the importance of faith in overcoming fear. Their letters to the early Christian communities encouraged believers to remain steadfast in their faith, even when faced with persecution. Paul's letters, such as his epistles to the Corinthians and the Ephesians, emphasize the importance of spiritual strength and unity. He encouraged believers to put on the "armor of God" and stand firm against the forces of evil (Ephesians 6:10-18). This metaphorical language served as a powerful reminder of the spiritual battle that Christians were engaged in and of the need for unwavering faith.

Jesus' teachings on God's constant care

A profound source of comfort to us in the midst of political fear is found in Jesus' teachings, particularly in the Sermon on the Mount. Jesus speaks directly to the worries that often consume us:

> *"Therefore I tell you, do not worry about your life, what you will eat or drink; or about your body, what you will wear. Is not life more than food, and the body more than clothes? Look at the birds of the air; they do not sow or reap or store away in barns, and yet your heavenly Father feeds them. Are you not much more valuable than they? Can any one of you by worrying add a single hour to your life?*
>
> *"And why do you worry about clothes? See how the flowers of the field grow. They do not labor or spin. Yet I tell you that not even Solomon in all his splendor was dressed like one of these. If that is how God clothes the grass of the field, which is here today and tomorrow is thrown into the fire, will he not much more clothe you—you of little faith? So do not worry, saying, 'What shall we eat?' or 'What shall we drink?' or 'What shall we wear?' For the pagans run after all these things, and your heavenly Father knows that you need them. But seek first his kingdom and his righteousness, and all these things will be given to you as well. Therefore, do not worry about tomorrow, for tomorrow will worry about itself. Each day has enough trouble of its own."*
> (Matthew 6:25-34).

In this passage, Jesus encourages us to trust in God's provision, reminding us that if God cares for the birds and the flowers, how much more will He care for us? In my counseling sessions, I often invite individuals to look out the window and observe any birds in flight. This simple act serves as a tangible reminder that God is always at work, providing for His creation, including us.

Practices for individual Christians to address political fear

As we continue to navigate the challenges of life, let us remember the words of Jesus, *"Do not worry about tomorrow, for tomorrow will worry about itself.*

Each day has enough trouble of its own." By trusting in God and supporting one another, we can face the future with confidence and hope.

Consider the following practices that Christians can take to help each other overcome anxiety and fear:

- **Pray and meditate.** Encourage regular prayer and meditation on Scripture. Praying together and reflecting on God's promises can bring peace and reassurance.
- **Share testimonies.** Share personal testimonies of God's faithfulness. Hearing how God has worked in the lives of others can strengthen faith and offer hope.
- **Provide access to counseling and support groups.** Professional counseling combined with spiritual guidance through the church can be particularly effective.
- **Engage in service and outreach.** Helping others can shift focus away from personal anxieties and foster a sense of purpose and connection.
- **Encourage healthy habits.** Promote healthy habits such as regular exercise, proper nutrition, and sufficient rest. Physical well-being can significantly impact mental and emotional health.

The role of the Church in addressing fear

In a time of increasing political concerns—whether about change, loss, others, or the unknown—the Church is called to maintain its focus on being a compassionate and Christ-centered presence. This calling involves Scriptural foundations, a prophetic voice, and theological reflection on the Church's mission.

Scriptural foundations for the Church's role

The Bible provides a strong foundation for the Church's role in addressing political fear. We are reminded of what the Lord requires, *"To act justly and to love mercy and to walk humbly with your God."* (Micah 6:8). This verse encapsulates the Church's call to justice, compassion, and humility.

Jesus' teachings also emphasize the importance of caring for the marginalized and standing against injustice. In Matthew 25:31-46, Jesus speaks of the final judgment and the importance of caring for "the least of these." This passage highlights the Church's responsibility to care for those who are vulnerable and oppressed.

The prophetic voice of the Church

The Church has a prophetic role in society, calling people to live according to God's standards of justice, mercy, and humility. This involves speaking out against fear-driven policies and actions that harm individuals and communities. The prophetic voice of the Church should offer hope and direction, reminding people of God's sovereignty and His call to love and justice.

In the Old Testament, prophets like Isaiah, Jeremiah, and Amos spoke out against the injustices and fears of their time. They called the people of Israel to repent and return to God, emphasizing the importance of justice and righteousness. Similarly, the Church today is called to be a voice of truth and love in a fearful and divided world.

Theological reflections on the Church's mission

The Church's mission is to be a light in the world, reflecting the love and justice of God. This involves not only preaching the Gospel but also living out its implications in practical ways. The Church is called to be a community that embodies the values of the Kingdom of God, including love, justice, and peace.

The concept of the "Kingdom of God" is central to the Church's mission. The Kingdom of God is a vision of a world where God's will is done on earth as it is in heaven. This vision includes justice for the oppressed, care for the marginalized, and the overcoming of fear and division.

Guidelines for churches to address political fear

Churches can implement the following guidelines to address political fear:

- **Educate and equip congregations.** Provide resources and training to help congregants understand the politics of fear and how to respond biblically. This can include sermons, Bible studies, and workshops.

- **Engage in advocacy.** Advocate for policies that promote justice and protect the rights of the vulnerable. This can involve working with other churches and organizations to amplify your voice.
- **Offer support and care.** Provide practical support and care for those affected by fear-driven policies, such as refugees, immigrants, and marginalized communities. This can include offering sanctuary, legal assistance, and other forms of support.
- **Foster unity and reconciliation.** Promote unity and reconciliation within the church and the wider community. This can involve facilitating dialogues, building relationships, and working towards healing and understanding.
- **Pray and seek God's guidance.** Regularly pray for wisdom, courage, and guidance in addressing political fear. Seek God's direction for how your church can be a light in the midst of darkness.

Examples of the Church's response to political fear

Faith communities played a central role in multiple movements of the twentieth century—namely the Anti-Apartheid Movement, the fall of communism in Eastern Europe, the Sanctuary Movement, and the Civil Rights Movement.

Each movement revealed forms of political idolatry in distinct ways: Apartheid prioritized race and authority; Communism emphasized the state; and U.S. segregation upheld a system of racial hierarchy.

Faith played a central role in these movements that were grounded in hope and vision. They succeeded due to grassroots organizing and community cohesion, not because of one individual.

The Anti-Apartheid movement, 1960s

In South Africa, churches were instrumental in the struggle against apartheid. Leaders like Desmond Tutu used their platforms to speak out against the injustice and fear perpetuated by the apartheid regime. The church provided a moral and spiritual framework for the movement, emphasizing the dignity and equality of all people.

The Sanctuary Movement, 1980s

Churches in the United States and Canada provided sanctuary to Central American refugees fleeing violence and persecution. The Sanctuary Movement was a response to fear-driven immigration policies and sought to protect the rights and dignity of refugees. The movement was grounded in the biblical mandate to care for the stranger and the oppressed.

The fall of communism in Eastern Europe, 1980s and 1990s

The Church played a vital role in supporting the people of Russia who were suffering under communist rule and the suppression of religious freedom. During this period, many individuals sought solace and placed their faith in God through Jesus Christ, desperately calling for Bibles and for those who would teach the word and way of Jesus Christ.[24]

International Bible societies responded to this need by discreetly sending Bibles to hidden house churches and congregations in Russia. These efforts were often carried out in secret to avoid detection by the authorities. Additionally, persecuted Christians received meaningful support from organizations such as Voice of the Martyrs. This group, founded and led by Richard and Sabina Wurmbrand, who themselves had suffered under communist regimes, provided spiritual, emotional, and physical support to those facing persecution.[25]

The Christian church's unwavering support over time empowered persecuted Christians in Russia to advocate for their rights and helped create international pressure against the oppressive communist regime. This advocacy was instrumental in the eventual fall of communism in Eastern Europe, as it highlighted the regime's human rights abuses and garnered global attention and condemnation.

The Civil Rights Movement, 1950s and 1960s

The Civil Rights Movement of the 1950s and 1960s was a turbulent and transformative period in American history. It was a time of intense struggle, marked by both incredible progress and profound resistance. The

---

[24] Ramet, S. P. (1998). Nihil Obstat: Religion, Politics, and Social Change in East-Central Europe and Russia. Duke University Press.

[25] Ibid

efforts of peacemakers from the Christian Church were crucial in ensuring that this period did not descend into greater chaos and violence.

Many churches and Christian leaders played a crucial role in the American Civil Rights Movement. They used their prophetic voice to speak out against racial injustice and to call for equality and human rights. The movement was rooted in the biblical principles of justice and love, and it drew strength from the faith and courage of its leaders and participants.

Dr. Martin Luther King Jr. and nonviolent protest

One of the most prominent figures during this time was Dr. Martin Luther King Jr., a Baptist minister who became the face of nonviolent resistance against racial injustice. Dr. King advocated for peaceful protest and civil disobedience, drawing on the teachings of Jesus Christ and Mahatma Gandhi. His philosophy was put to the test as he faced numerous threats to his life for his unwavering stand for the equal treatment of Black people under the United States Constitution. Despite the constant danger, Dr. King remained steadfast in his commitment to nonviolence, believing it to be the most powerful tool for social change.

Other Christian leaders and their sacrifices

Dr. King was not alone in his struggle. Other Christian leaders also faced threats, physical assault, and even death for the cause of justice.

- **Dr. James Farmer**, one of the founders of the Congress of Racial Equality (CORE), was a key figure in organizing the Freedom Rides to challenge segregation in interstate travel.
- **Fannie Lou Hamer**, a deeply religious woman, became a powerful voice in the fight for voting rights and endured severe beatings and imprisonment for her activism.
- **Medgar Evers**, a field secretary for the NAACP, worked tirelessly to end segregation and was tragically assassinated for his efforts.

Personal connection to community support and rebuilding

This era holds special significance for me due to my parents' church ministry and their involvement in the Civil Rights Movement. My mother, while a college student, participated in the Student Nonviolent Coordinating Committee (SNCC). She was involved in restaurant counter sit-ins that drew national attention to the violation of civil rights in access to public places of business. Her courageous actions helped to highlight the injustices faced by African Americans and spurred action towards greater equality.

My father, a minister in the African Methodist Episcopal Zion (AMEZ) Church, led his congregation through the aftermath of a devastating arson attack. Our church was burned down, with evidence of candles and kerosene pointing to an intentional act of hate. Despite this, my father and mother remained resolute in their faith and commitment to justice. In recounting the incident, my father said, "We saw candles that were lit, and where kerosene was poured through the church." This could have easily been a moment where fear and animosity took hold, but the response from the community was a blessing![26]

In the face of such adversity, the community rallied together. The Quakers, known for their commitment to peace and social justice, volunteered their time and resources to help clear the debris from the burned church. Their selfless actions demonstrated the power of solidarity and compassion in times of crisis.

A local White Methodist congregation, Wayside Methodist Church in Tinton Falls, NJ, extended an invitation to our church to join them for Easter worship and offered the use of their facilities. This act of kindness and inclusion was a powerful testament to the Christian principles of love and fellowship.

Moreover, a wealthy resident from the community made a significant donation of $5,000 (a considerable sum in 1964) towards the reconstruction of our church. This generous act underscored the importance of support and generosity in overcoming hate and rebuilding hope. The collective efforts of the Christian Church and the broader community during the Civil

---

[26] *Apr 07, 1969, page 1 - The Daily Register at.* (n.d.). Newspapers.com. Retrieved November 18, 2024, from https://www.newspapers.com/image/516986255/?match=1&terms=Rev.%20Charles%20Lee%20Clemons

Rights Movement played a crucial role in alleviating fear and hate, and in bringing about peace and justice.

The following article from 1969 highlights the devastation to the Reevytown Church and the act of kindness extended by the Wayside Methodist church in the shadows of Dr. King's death anniversary:

King Death Anniversary Marked in Red Bank

SEE STORY BELOW

Fair, Pleasant

THE DAILY **REGISTER**

FINAL EDITION

VOL. 91, NO. 199   RED BANK, N.J., MONDAY, APRIL 7, 1969   22 PAGES   10 CENTS

Monmouth County's Home Newspaper for 90 Years

Wayside Methodists Share Service With Victims

Reevytown Church Fire Seen 'Definite' Arson

Say Curbs Ruled Out Viet Military Victory

FIRE'S TOLL — The Rev. Charles Lee Clemons, pastor of the Reevytown A.M.E. Zion Church, New Shrewsbury, shows Walter B. Cobb Jr., borough fire marshal, 100-year-old Bible charred by fire which wrecked interior of 85-year-old church early Saturday. Mr. Cobb says the fire was "definitely set."

(Register Staff Photo)

Chapter 8: Conspiracy theories and the Christian response

A conspiracy theory claims that a secret group secretly causes significant events, usually without verifiable evidence. It's sometimes based on undisclosed motives, limited evidence, or assumptions.

For as long as humanity has sought to understand the complexities of life, there have been efforts to explain the inexplicable. In times of uncertainty, fear, and division, conspiracy theories often rise as seductive narratives, offering a sense of control, clarity, and purpose. Yet these theories, while appearing insightful, often entangle minds in shadows, distort truth, and lead to harmful consequences.

Conspiracy theories thrive on suspicion, often painting powerful institutions or marginalized groups as malevolent actors. These theories exploit fear by suggesting that nothing is as it seems, and that unseen forces manipulate the world for their gain. In times of crisis, misinformation can spread as quickly as the disease itself. Conspiracy theories exploit fear, thereby fostering division and distraction from the real work of addressing suffering.

This chapter explores the origins and functions of conspiracy theories, highlighting their fallacies and dangers. It also contrasts these with biblical principles that guide believers to discern truth and resist paranoia. Through examples across history, we will see how the wisdom of Scripture provides clarity and stability in a world prone to confusion.

How to identify a conspiracy theory

It's important to be able to identify conspiracy theories. Ask yourself the following questions before you believe a theory:

- Does the theory makes extraordinary claims?
- Does the theory appeal to emotion and panic?
- Is the story vague about the parties involved or the logistics of the theory?

- Has the narrative evolved as it's retold?
- Are the motives questionable?
- Is there an absence of verifiable evidence, such as documents or dependable witnesses?

If you answer "yes" to any of the above questions, you're likely hearing a conspiracy theory.

Origins and functions of conspiracy theories

Conspiracy theories are not a modern phenomenon; their roots stretch back to ancient civilizations, persist through the Middle Ages, and continue into the digital age. For Christians, these narratives present a particular challenge. They are not merely intellectual distractions; they are fundamentally at odds with the biblical call to truth, peace, and trust in God.

Conspiracy theories often arise in times of crisis when people seek explanations for events that defy simple understanding. This psychological tendency stems from the human need for meaning, particularly in chaotic or threatening situations. When faced with fear or uncertainty, individuals are drawn to narratives that provide:

- **Cohesion.** A clear story that connects disparate events.
- **Agency.** A sense of control by identifying culprits or forces behind events.
- **Belonging.** A community of like-minded believers united against a perceived enemy.

The fallacies of conspiracy theories

It's important to understand the fallacies of conspiracy theories, including over-simplification, disproof, and distrust.

- **The fallacy of over-simplification.** Conspiracy theories often reduce complex events to simplistic narratives. During the Black Death in the 14th century, a deadly conspiracy theory spread across Europe claiming that Jewish communities had intentionally caused the plague by poisoning wells in order to kill Christians. This baseless theory fueled violent massacres.

- **The fallacy of disproof.** Conspiracy theories are designed to resist disproof. Evidence against the theory is often dismissed as part of the conspiracy itself. For example, in modern times, the "moon landing hoax" theory persists despite overwhelming evidence. Proponents claim that NASA's evidence is fabricated, creating a circular argument. Note that all theories related to this "hoax" have been debunked through scientific explanations.

- **The fallacy of distrust.** Conspiracy theories erode trust in institutions, experts, and even neighbors. For example, during the COVID-19 pandemic, theories about vaccine microchips led to widespread hesitancy, undermining public health efforts and prolonging the crisis.

Conspiracy theories throughout the ages

Consider some examples of conspiracy theories that had side effects such as scapegoating, fear of disease, us-versus-them mentality, and distrust in institutions.

Ancient examples

- **The assassination of Julius Caesar (44 BC).** The conspiracy to assassinate Caesar sparked widespread paranoia in Rome, culminating in the eventual rise of Augustus as emperor. The subsequent political turmoil demonstrates how conspiracies often lead to unintended consequences.

- **The Great Fire of Rome (AD 64).** After the devastating fire that consumed much of Rome, rumors spread that Emperor Nero had deliberately set the city ablaze to make room for his grand architectural ambitions. Nero deflected blame by accusing Christians, leading to intense persecution. This early conspiracy theory illustrates how fear and suspicion can justify oppression and sow division.

Historic examples

- **The witch hunts (Middle ages).** In medieval Europe, conspiracy theories about witches colluding with the devil led to mass hysteria and thousands of executions. These events highlight the dangers of scapegoating and the tragic consequences of baseless accusations.

- **Black Death bioterrorism (14th century).** The destructive Black Death of the 14th century has stimulated theories suggesting that it was a deliberate act of bioterrorism. There were claims of well-poisoning and deliberate spread of the plague, contributing to various theories surrounding one of history's deadliest pandemics.

Modern-day examples

- **The Protocols of the Elders of Zion (20th century).** The Protocols of the Elders of Zion is a fabricated text stating a detailed Jewish plot for global domination. This fraudulent document, along with Nazi propaganda, aimed to reveal a Jewish conspiracy to dominate the world fueled antisemitism. It underscores how conspiracy theories can have devastating real-world impacts.

- **Digital amplification (modern era).** In the modern era, social media supercharged conspiracy theories, providing platforms for rapid dissemination and reinforcement. Movements like QAnon, which alleges hidden networks of global elites controlling society, exemplify how these narratives flourish in echo chambers where critical thinking is replaced by confirmation bias.

- **Autism.** In the late 20th century, when *The Lancet* published an article suggesting a connection between childhood vaccines and autism, the author was fired from the UK medical register, and the article was retracted. Analysis and large-scale studies consistently find no causal link, yet people continue to believe the theory, perpetuate it, and fight against life-saving vaccines for their children.

    Recently, the HHS announced that Tylenol ingested by pregnant women and babies causes autism. This finding was formed by a group of non-medical professionals without any research or proof. The FDA posted a notice responding about a possible association, noting that association is not the same as causation.[27] At the publishing of this book, it's too early to know if this theory will be accepted or rejected by the public.

---

[27] FDA News Release, https://www.fda.gov/news-events/press-announcements/fda-responds-evidence-possible-association-between-autism-and-acetaminophen-use-during-pregnancy

The Bible's counterweight to conspiracy theories

The Bible provides us with Scripture to counterbalance conspiracy theories.

God is the source of truth

Scripture anchors believers in the truth of God's sovereignty and character by reminding us, *"For God is not a God of disorder but of peace."* (1 Corinthians 14:33). In contrast to the chaos and paranoia of conspiracy theories, God offers clarity, light, and peace. Aligning our minds with His Word enables us to discern truth from deception.

Believers are called to *"Trust in the Lord with all your heart and lean not on your own understanding."*(Proverbs 3:5–6).While conspiracy theories appeal to human reasoning, Christians are called to place their trust in God's omniscience and providence.

Satan is the source of lies and deception

Jesus identifies Satan as the "father of lies" (John 8:44). Conspiracy theories often mirror Satan's tactics by:

- Distorting reality to sow doubt.
- Exploiting fear to manipulate behavior.
- Creating division and hostility.

A Christian response to conspiracy theories

Conspiracy theories thrive in darkness, feeding on fear and distrust. For Christians, the antidote is clear: a steadfast commitment to God's truth, revealed in Scripture, and a life marked by faith, peace, and love. The Bible contains Scripture that identifies the Christian response to conspiracy theories:

- **Seek truth in Scripture.** Believers must ground themselves in God's Word, which provides clarity amid confusion. *"Your word is a lamp to my feet and a light to my path."* (Psalm 119:105).
- **Cultivate discernment.** Christians are called to be wise and discerning, focusing on God's truth rather than rumors. Proverbs 3:5–6 reminds believers to trust in the Lord with all their hearts, leaning

not on their own understanding. They're also called to test everything against Scripture (1 Thessalonians 5:21). This includes evaluating news, claims, and narratives with wisdom and critical thinking.

- **Promote peace and unity.** Conspiracy theories often breed division. Christians are peacemakers, called to build bridges rather than walls. Jesus tells us, *"Blessed are the peacemakers, for they will be called children of God."* (Matthew 5:9). Philippians 2:1–2 tells us that faith unites us. By rejecting conspiracy thinking, Christians can build bridges of trust and compassion.

- **Trust God's sovereignty.** Ultimately, believers can rest in the assurance that God is in control. Conspiracy theories prey on fear, but Scripture reminds us, *"Do not fear, for I am with you; do not be dismayed, for I am your God."* (Isaiah 41:10).

In a world captivated by shadows, let us be children of the light, proclaiming the truth of the Gospel and trusting in the One who holds all things together.

Chapter 9: A Christian response to fears of disease and death

From the 2022 Chapman University survey, we saw that around 60% of the participants were afraid or very afraid of disease and death. But the fear of disease and death is nothing new—it's as old as humanity itself. From ancient epidemics to modern pandemics, the specter of illness and mortality has haunted individuals and communities alike. For Christians, these fears present profound challenges and opportunities to confront uncertainty with faith, to respond to suffering with compassion, and to resist despair with the hope of eternal life.

Examples of responses to disease and death

Let's explore both the historical and contemporary responses of Christians to disease and death, the dangers of misinformation, and the powerful example set by Jesus Christ and His followers. While fear is a natural reaction, it is through faith in God's sovereignty and promises that believers can find strength and peace.

Compassion: Leprosy in Biblical times

Leprosy, one of the most feared diseases of the ancient world, carried immense social and spiritual stigma. In the Old Testament, lepers were isolated, living outside the community and often seen as cursed by God. Yet even in this context, God's mercy was evident.

- **The prophets' response.** The story of Naaman and Elisha in 2 Kings 5 reveals God's power over disease and His concern for the afflicted. Naaman's healing was not only physical but also spiritual, a testimony to God's compassion.
- **Jesus' radical ministry.** Jesus' encounters with lepers challenged societal norms. He touched and healed those considered untouchable, demonstrating that God's love transcends human prejudice

(Matthew 8:1–4, Luke 17:11–19). His example calls Christians to respond to disease with empathy rather than fear.

Sacrificial love: The Black Death in the Middle Ages

During the Black Death that claimed millions of lives across Europe, Christians faced a choice to flee in fear or to stay and serve. Many chose the latter, embodying Christ's call to love one's neighbor.

- **Acts of courage.** Christian communities provided care for the dying, often at great personal risk. Their actions reflected the sacrificial love of Christ.
- **Martin Luther's leadership.** During a plague in Wittenberg, Martin Luther emphasized faith and service. In his writings, he balanced precaution with trust in God, encouraging believers to act wisely while still supporting those in need.

Compassion amid stigma: The HIV/AIDS crisis in the 1980s

The HIV/AIDS epidemic brought new challenges for Christians. Fear and misinformation led to widespread discrimination against those affected, often compounding their suffering.

- **Fearful responses.** Sadly, some Christians viewed AIDS as divine punishment, failing to show the compassion exemplified by Jesus.
- **A different way.** Others, like Mother Hale, responded with love and care. Her work with AIDS-infected babies in Harlem demonstrated that faith in action can overcome stigma and fear.
- **Personal reflections.** On a personal note, my early ministry work included serving at a summer camp for families affected by HIV/AIDS. There, I witnessed the beauty of dedication ceremonies for children and the renewal of vows by couples affected by the virus. Despite the challenges, these individuals demonstrated a profound commitment to their faith and to each other.

Courage in the face of crisis: Ebola outbreak in 2018

Ebola outbreaks in West Africa highlighted the urgency of responding to medical emergencies with both courage and compassion. Christians, particularly healthcare workers, played pivotal roles.

- **Recognizing legitimate threats.** While fear of Ebola was justified, panic was not. Christians supported efforts to combat the disease through accurate information and medical care.
- **Unified action.** Collaboration between faith communities, healthcare professionals, and governments was essential. The courage of healthcare workers, often motivated by faith, was a testament to God's sustaining power.

A divided response: COVID-19 pandemic in 2020

The COVID-19 pandemic revealed the complexities of responding to a global crisis in a deeply polarized world.

- **Political divisions.** The pandemic became a battleground for competing ideologies. Some prioritized public health measures as acts of love, while others resisted the measures as infringements on personal liberties.
- **Misinformation and fear.** Conspiracy theories thrived, creating confusion and distrust. Christians were called to discern truth and reject fear-based narratives.
- **Compassionate responses.** Many believers stepped forward to provide practical help, emotional support, and prayer. Their actions mirrored the early Church's care for the vulnerable.

Overcome fear through faith

Throughout history, Christians have faced the crippling fears of disease and death with faith, courage, and compassion. By looking to Jesus Christ, who overcame death itself, believers find the strength to confront their fears and serve a hurting world.

Maintain the Christian perspective on death

For believers, death is not the end. The resurrection of Jesus Christ transforms death from a source of fear to a doorway to eternal life.

- **Hope in eternity.** Jesus' promise in John 14:1–3 assures Christians of a place in His Father's house. This hope empowers believers to face death with courage.

- **Freedom from fear.** Hebrews 2:14–15 declares that Christ has freed humanity from the fear of death, breaking its power through His victory on the cross.

Keep faith in crisis

Let us live as people of hope, trusting in the God who reigns over all and proclaiming His love through our words and actions.

- **Seek God's word.** Scripture provides clarity and comfort in times of uncertainty. Passages like Psalm 23 remind believers of God's presence, even in the valley of the shadow of death.
- **Show compassion.** Following Jesus' example, Christians are called to serve those affected by disease, demonstrating His love through practical acts of kindness.
- **Trust God's sovereignty.** In the face of global uncertainty, Psalm 46:1–2 declares, *"God is our refuge and strength, an ever-present help in trouble. Therefore we will not fear."*

As Scripture reminds us, *"Nothing can separate us from the love of God that is in Christ Jesus our Lord."* (Romans 8:38–39).

Live with hope and compassion

The following guidelines for living with hope and compassion can help to starve fear by feeding the faith:

- **Balance precaution with faith.** Martin Luther's approach during the plague remains a model for Christians today. Taking reasonable precautions while trusting God reflects a balanced and faithful response.
- **Keep the eternal perspective.** Disease and death are temporary realities in a fallen world. Revelation 21:4 offers a vision of a future where *"there will be no more death or mourning or crying or pain."*
- **Build a legacy of love.** From the early Church's care for lepers to modern responses to pandemics, Christians have shown that faith overcomes fear when grounded in God's love. By trusting in His promises and serving others, believers can leave a lasting impact on a fearful world.

Chapter 10: Fear of government corruption

The 2022 survey found that about 70% of people feared government corruption, a concern that dates back to early civilization. In the biblical account of Exodus, the Israelites experienced political fear firsthand under a new pharaoh who didn't know Joseph. Pharaoh, fearing the growing numbers and strength of the Israelites, weaponized fear to justify their enslavement. His strategy was simple yet insidious, to portray the Israelites as a threat to national security.

> *Behold, the people of Israel are too many and too mighty for us. Come, let us deal shrewdly with them, lest they multiply, and, if war breaks out, they join our enemies and fight against us and escape from the land."* (Exodus 1:9-10).

The parallels to modern political rhetoric are striking. Governments faced with internal or external crises often manufacture or exaggerate threats to justify draconian measures. In doing so, they foster an atmosphere of distrust and fear. Like the Israelites, many communities today find themselves targeted by policies rooted in fear rather than justice.

The Christian response to such fear is to trust in God's ultimate authority. Just as God delivered the Israelites from Pharaoh's oppressive regime, so too does He promise justice for all nations.

The legacy of fascism: Mussolini, Hitler, and the politics of fear

The 20th century saw fear elevated to an art form under fascist regimes. Benito Mussolini and Adolf Hitler rose to power by exploiting the anxieties of their respective nations. Mussolini tapped into Italy's disillusionment after World War I, presenting himself as the strongman who could restore order and national pride. Hitler, in turn, capitalized on Germany's post-war humiliation and economic despair, using fear of "the other"—Jews, Communists, and other minority groups—to consolidate his power.

Fascism thrives on the promise of protection in exchange for obedience. Mussolini famously declared, "Everything within the state, nothing outside the state, nothing against the state." Hitler echoed this sentiment with his concept of *Führerprinzip*, the idea that absolute authority rests in the hands of a singular leader.

Today, echoes of fascist ideology can be seen in groups like the Proud Boys and Oath Keepers who promote authoritarianism under the guise of nationalism and self-defense. In order to mobilize their followers, these organizations leverage fear of immigration, governmental overreach, and cultural change.

Anti-fascism: Stjepan Filipović and the modern antifa movement

Not all succumbed to fear during the rise of fascism. Resistance movements such as antifa emerged across Europe, often at great personal cost. One of the most iconic figures of this resistance is Stjepan Filipović, a Yugoslav partisan fighter who defied fascist forces during World War II. Captured and executed by the Nazis, Filipović faced his death with arms outstretched and a cry for freedom, "Death to fascism, freedom to the people!" His bravery serves as a testament to the power of hope and resistance in the face of tyranny.

In the modern era, groups like antifa claim to carry forward this legacy of anti-fascism. While controversial in their methods, these movements position themselves as defenders against the resurgence of authoritarian ideologies. Critics argue that their tactics sometimes mirror the violence they oppose, raising questions about whether such resistance aligns with biblical principles of peace and justice.

For Christians, the lesson is clear: taking a stand against injustice is required by biblical teaching, but the approach must reflect the character of Christ. Faith-based resistance aims to achieve justice without continuing patterns of fear or violence.

God's sovereignty: The Christian response to fear

Consider the stark contrast to the chaos of human governance. The psalmist declares that God's reign is characterized by justice, righteousness, and equity:

"The Lord reigns; let the nations tremble! He sits enthroned between the cherubim – let the earth shake. Great is the Lord in Zion; He is exalted over all the nations." (Psalm 99).

This vision of divine sovereignty stands in opposition to the fear-driven rule of earthly powers. For Christians, this means placing ultimate trust not in governments or movements but in God's eternal rule.

While human leaders may fail, God's justice is unchanging. This trust frees Christians from the paralyzing fear of corruption, persecution, or societal collapse. It also calls believers to be agents of peace and reconciliation, demonstrating an alternative to the fear and division that dominate political discourse.

Faith over fear

The politics of fear is nothing new, nor is God's call to faith. From the oppression of Pharaoh to the rise of fascist regimes, history is filled with examples of fear being used to control and divide. Yet, in every generation, there are those who choose faith over fear, trusting in God's sovereignty and justice.

For Christians, it's essential to navigate a world rife with political fear without losing sight of God's eternal reign. Psalm 99 reminds us that the Lord is on His throne and that His justice will prevail. By living in this truth, we can confront the politics of fear with courage, hope, and love.

Chapter 11: Cultivate hope, empathy, and forgiveness

Hope, empathy, and forgiveness are powerful emotional tools for overcoming fear, such as fear rooted in pain, conflict, or mistrust. Overcoming fear doesn't always mean erasing it; it means having the emotional strength to move forward despite it.

Each emotion responds to fear in a unique but connected way, and together, they help us shift from a mindset of survival to one of healing and growth. Hope helps us face what's ahead. Empathy helps us face what we don't understand. Forgiveness helps us face what's wounded us.

Cultivate hope

The theology of hope begins with a re-examination of the very definition of hope. It is not passive wishing, a wistful longing for a better tomorrow. Hope, as understood within a robust Christian framework, is an active, engaged posture, a confident expectation rooted in the character of God and the promises of Scripture. It is the confident anticipation of God's ultimate victory over evil, a victory that is already begun in the resurrection of Jesus Christ. This hope isn't simply a feeling; it's a conviction that shapes our actions, our choices, and our interactions with the world.

This hope is not confined to the individual; it spills over into the social and political realms. It compels us to work for justice, to fight against oppression, and to build a world that reflects God's love and compassion. This is not a naïve utopianism; it's a pragmatic engagement with the world, fueled by the conviction that God is at work, even amid chaos and suffering. It necessitates discernment, a careful weighing of actions and consequences, an understanding of the complexities of the political landscape. However, it never loses sight of the ultimate goal – a world redeemed, transformed, and reconciled to God.

Examine your anxieties

Developing a theology of hope requires a careful examination of our own anxieties and fears. We must honestly confront the sources of our fear to identify those things that hold us captive and prevent us from embracing the fullness of God's promises. This self-reflection may be uncomfortable, but it's a necessary step in the process of liberation. It demands a willingness to examine the ways in which our fears have shaped our beliefs, our actions, and our relationships. It requires confronting the ways in which fear has been manipulated and weaponized in the political sphere, from the rise of Christian nationalism to the spread of misinformation and conspiracy theories.

After we identify the root of our fears, we can begin the process of healing and transformation. This requires engaging with the Scriptures not passively but actively, allowing the word of God to penetrate our hearts and minds, renewing our perspectives and challenging our assumptions. It involves engaging in spiritual disciplines such as prayer, meditation, and worship, allowing ourselves to be filled with the peace and strength that comes from God's presence.

Cultivate practices that nurture hope

Crucially, we must also actively cultivate practices that nurture hope. This may involve participating in acts of service, volunteering in our communities, and working for social justice. It may involve engaging in creative expression, finding ways to express our faith through art, music, literature, or other creative endeavors. It may involve connecting with others who share our faith, finding strength and encouragement in the company of fellow believers. In all of these practices, we are not merely attempting to alleviate our own anxieties; we are actively participating in God's redemptive work in the world.

Confront the nature of hopelessness

The cultivation of hope also necessitates a confrontation with the insidious nature of despair. Despair, often subtly masked as realism or pragmatism, is the antithesis of hope. It's the voice that whispers, "It's all futile," "Nothing will ever change," "It's too late." This voice is often amplified by the relentless negativity of the media and the cynicism that pervades our political landscape. To combat this despair, we must actively cultivate a narrative that counters it, a narrative grounded in the unwavering faithfulness of God and the ultimate triumph of good over evil.

This narrative is not a denial of suffering, but an affirmation that even amidst suffering, God is present, God is active, and God is working toward redemption. It is a narrative that emphasizes God's steadfast love, a love that is not shaken by our failures or the failures of the world. It is a narrative that reminds us that God's promises are sure, even when the path to their fulfillment is long and arduous.

Engage in the political landscape

This hope, however, is not a passive resignation to fate. It fuels action. A true theology of hope compels us to engage actively in the political landscape, to challenge injustice, and to advocate for the marginalized and vulnerable. This engagement is rooted not in anger or resentment, but in a profound conviction that God is calling us to participate in the building of a more just and equitable world. This might involve advocating for policy changes, supporting organizations working for social justice, or simply engaging in respectful dialogue with those who hold differing viewpoints. The crucial aspect is to approach these political engagements with a spirit of grace, humility, and a persistent hope for reconciliation (Micah 6:8).

This engagement must be rooted in love, recognizing the inherent dignity of all human beings, regardless of their beliefs or political affiliations. This doesn't mean compromising values or neglecting to challenge injustice. It means **interacting with others respectfully and empathetically, aiming to find shared interests when you can, and working towards resolution even when major differences exist.** The goal is not to win arguments, but to build bridges, to foster understanding, and to cultivate a culture of mutual respect.

Furthermore, our engagement with the political landscape should be informed by the historical context of Christianity. Throughout its history, Christianity has wrestled with the complexities of power, oppression, and social injustice. There have been times when Christians have failed to live up to their calling, succumbing to the temptations of power and violence. But there have also been countless examples of Christians who have actively resisted oppression, championed the cause of the poor and marginalized, and worked tirelessly for justice and peace. Learning from both the successes and failures of the past, we can develop a more nuanced and effective approach to political engagement in the present.

Trust in God's sovereignty

Finally, cultivating a theology of hope requires a profound trust in God's sovereignty and providence. This isn't a passive fatalism, but a confident acknowledgment that God is in control, even when things seem chaotic and unpredictable. It's the knowledge that God's plan is greater than our understanding, and that even suffering can be used for good.

This trust allows us to move beyond fear and anxiety, embracing the challenges of life with courage and faith, knowing that *"God works for the good of those who love him."* (Romans 8:28). This trust, coupled with a resolute commitment to justice and love, forms the foundation of a truly transformative theology of hope—a hope that not only sustains us in the face of adversity but also empowers us to build a culture of faith that transcends fear. It is this hope that will ultimately allow us to build a community, a nation, and a world where faith prevails, and love conquers all.

Examples of hope

The Old Testament is replete with examples of hope in the face of overwhelming adversity. Consider Abraham, called to leave his homeland and journey to a promised land, a land he would never fully possess in his lifetime. His hope wasn't based on immediate gratification, but on a covenant with God, a promise whispered across centuries. Also, consider the Israelites in exile, their temple destroyed, their nation shattered. Yet, their prophets proclaimed a message of hope, a vision of restoration and redemption, a future where God's people would be gathered once more. This hope sustained them through unimaginable hardship, reminding them that God's promises, though delayed, were not forgotten.

The New Testament provides the ultimate expression of hope in the person and work of Jesus Christ. His life, death, and resurrection are not merely historical events; they are the foundation upon which our hope rests. Jesus, in the face of unimaginable suffering and injustice, offered a radical message of love, forgiveness, and reconciliation. His death on the cross wasn't a defeat, but a victory over the powers of darkness, a demonstration of God's unwavering love for a fallen world. His resurrection is the ultimate affirmation of hope, the guarantee of new life, both now and in the age to come.

Cultivate vulnerability and empathy

We've laid the groundwork for a theology of hope, a robust faith that transcends the anxieties of our time. But hope, vibrant and resilient as it may be, can't exist in a vacuum. It requires fertile ground, a soil nourished by empathy and vulnerability. Without these crucial elements, our hope remains an isolated flame, easily extinguished by the winds of political division. It is here, in the fertile ground of empathy and vulnerability, that our faith can truly blossom and bear the fruit of a more just and compassionate society.

Confront vulnerabilities

To build a culture of faith that transcends fear, we must first confront our own vulnerabilities. This isn't a sign of weakness, but of profound strength. It is in acknowledging our own imperfections, our own capacity for error and prejudice, that we create space for genuine connection with others.

Vulnerability is not a weakness. It's not about laying bare our souls to every person we encounter; it's about building trust in carefully chosen settings, allowing ourselves to be seen and understood in our entirety. This means being authentic, accepting our imperfections, and not being afraid to admit when we are wrong.

Think of the parable of the Good Samaritan in Luke 10:30-37. The priest and the Levite, likely driven by fear of contamination or possibly being robbed, passed by the wounded man. The Samaritan, however, risked his own safety and social standing to show compassion. He chose vulnerability, and in that vulnerability, he demonstrated the very essence of love.

This act of vulnerability, a willingness to expose oneself to potential harm or criticism, is crucial for bridging the vast chasms of political division. We have spent too much time rooted in our own ideologies, exchanging harsh words and accusations across the divide of disagreement. We've forgotten the power of listening, of truly hearing the stories and perspectives of those who hold opposing views. We've become so consumed by the need to be right, so invested in defending our own positions, that we've lost sight of the shared humanity that binds us together.

Nourish empathy

When we choose to listen, when we are willing to set aside our preconceived notions and enter into genuine dialogue, we begin to see the world through the eyes of others. We encounter the complexities of their experiences, the reasons behind their beliefs, and the fears that shape their perspectives. This is the essence of empathy: the capacity to understand and share the feelings of another. It's not necessarily agreeing with them, but truly seeing them—their hopes, their struggles, their humanity. It requires a humility that acknowledges our own limitations and a willingness to learn from others.

To cultivate empathy, we need to deliberately practice mindfulness. We need to pause before reacting, to take a deep breath and consider the perspective of the other person. We need to ask ourselves what their experiences have been, what their fears are, and what their hopes are for the future. This often requires us to confront our own biases, to acknowledge the ways in which our own experiences have shaped our perspectives, and to recognize that others' experiences might be profoundly different from our own.

Building bridges of understanding requires us to acknowledge the role of power dynamics. Often, the most marginalized voices are the ones least heard. We must actively create spaces for those voices to be amplified, to ensure that their experiences and perspectives are taken seriously. This involves actively listening, valuing their contributions, and working to dismantle systemic barriers that silence or marginalize them.

Foster authentic community

In our contemporary political landscape, where rhetoric is often heated and divisions are deep, the practice of empathy can feel almost revolutionary. We are bombarded daily with messages of fear and division, often designed to exploit our inherent biases and prejudices. Social media algorithms, designed to maximize engagement, frequently prioritize sensationalism and outrage over reasoned discourse. This creates an environment where empathy is often drowned out by noise and negativity.

Yet, it is precisely in this environment that the practice of vulnerability and empathy becomes most crucial. We need to actively cultivate these virtues, both within ourselves and within our communities. This requires a conscious effort to seek out diverse perspectives, to listen without judgment, and to engage in respectful dialogue, even when we disagree strongly. It means challenging ourselves to step outside our echo chambers and engage with those who hold different views. It may involve attending town halls and community forums where you may face uncomfortable questions or viewpoints that challenge your beliefs.

Furthermore, fostering vulnerability and empathy requires fostering authentic community. This isn't simply about gathering together for services or events; it's about building genuine relationships where individuals feel safe to share their experiences, their doubts, and their vulnerabilities without fear of judgment or condemnation. Such communities provide a nurturing environment where empathy can flourish, where individuals can learn to support each other and to face the challenges of life together.

The church, as a community of faith, has a vital role to play in cultivating the values of empathy and vulnerability. It should be a safe haven for honest conversations, a space where differing viewpoints can be expressed respectfully and where individuals can find support and encouragement in their journeys of faith. It's in these safe spaces, free from the toxic political rhetoric of our time, that hearts can soften, minds can open, and the transformative power of empathy can truly take hold.

It is through this commitment to vulnerability and empathy, coupled with a theology of hope, that we can build a culture of faith that truly transcends fear. A culture where our shared humanity outweighs our political differences, allowing us to work collaboratively toward a future of peace, justice, and love. This is not a utopian dream, but a challenge we must embrace—a testament to our faith and a reflection of the very nature of God.

Examples of vulnerability and empathy

The historical record is replete with examples of this principle in action. Consider the early Christians, often persecuted for their beliefs. Their response wasn't to retaliate with violence or to withdraw into isolation. Instead, many chose a path of radical love and compassion. They demonstrated vulnerability by openly sharing their faith in the face of hostility, offering forgiveness to their persecutors, and providing charity to the poor and marginalized—even those who actively opposed them. Their actions weren't naïve; they understood the risks involved. But their faith in a God of love propelled them to act, even in the face of significant danger.

The struggle for civil rights in the 20th century also provides a powerful illustration. The leaders of the Civil Rights Movement, from Martin Luther King Jr. to countless others who walked alongside him, showed extraordinary courage and vulnerability. They faced violence, intimidation, and imprisonment, but they persisted because they believed in a future where equality and justice would prevail. Their actions weren't fueled by hatred or a desire for revenge, but by a deep empathy for the suffering of their people and an unwavering belief in the transformative power of love. They were willing to expose themselves to the harsh realities of segregation and discrimination, not to win an argument, but to build a more just and inclusive society.

Cultivate forgiveness and reconciliation

The seeds of hope, sown in the fertile ground of empathy and vulnerability, must now be nurtured. This nurturing process demands a conscious, deliberate cultivation of forgiveness and reconciliation. Forgiveness and reconciliation aren't easy paths. They require grappling with complex emotions, confronting painful memories, and acknowledging the deep wounds inflicted by injustice.

Release bitterness to forgive

Forgiveness isn't a passive sentiment; it's an active, transformative force that dismantles the walls of fear and resentment erected by political division. It's a conscious choice to release the bitterness that festers in our hearts, a choice that requires courage, humility, and a profound understanding of our shared humanity. It's about recognizing the inherent dignity and worth of every human being, even those who have caused us harm. This isn't a call for naïve forgiveness, a blanket pardon for all transgressions. It's a call for discerning forgiveness, rooted in a deep understanding of justice and a commitment to healing.

Apply forgiveness to reconcile

Reconciliation, in turn, is the bridge that connects forgiveness to the restoration of broken relationships, both personal and societal. It's the painstaking work of rebuilding trust, fostering understanding, and finding common ground in the midst of profound disagreement.

Reconciliation, then, is the practical application of forgiveness. It demands courageous conversations, an honest acknowledgment of past wrongs, and a sincere commitment to making amends. This process often necessitates facing difficult truths, acknowledging complicity in systems of oppression, and committing to tangible actions that promote healing and justice. Reconciliation can't be imposed; it's a process that must be engaged voluntarily by all parties involved. It requires empathy, humility, and a willingness to listen deeply to the experiences of others, even when those experiences challenge our own perspectives.

In the political sphere, reconciliation translates to a commitment to dialogue, even with those with whom we deeply disagree. It's not a call for compromising our convictions but a call for respectful engagement, recognizing the humanity of those who hold different viewpoints. It's about finding common ground, focusing on shared values and goals, and resisting the temptation to demonize our opponents. Building bridges requires a willingness to listen, learn, and understand, setting aside preconceived notions and stereotypes.

The role of the Church in forgiveness and reconciliation

The Church, as a community committed to Christ's teachings, has a pivotal role to play in fostering a culture of forgiveness and reconciliation. It should be a space where difficult conversations can take place, where individuals can share their experiences of hurt and pain, and where the transformative power of forgiveness can heal deep wounds. This requires intentional community building, creating safe spaces for authentic dialogue, and providing opportunities for healing and restoration. In this setting, pastoral care plays a crucial role by providing guidance, support, and spiritual direction to those facing difficulties with anger, resentment, and forgiveness.

The Church's commitment to social justice is inherently intertwined with forgiveness and reconciliation. Addressing systemic injustices, advocating for the marginalized, and working towards a more just and equitable society are crucial components of the reconciliation process. True reconciliation requires not just individual forgiveness, but societal transformation. This involves challenging oppressive structures, promoting policies that address inequality, and creating communities where everyone can thrive. It demands engaging with the complexities of race, class, and power, acknowledging historical injustices and working actively towards a more just future.

But how do we navigate the complexities of forgiveness and reconciliation, particularly when dealing with deep-seated historical trauma and ongoing systemic injustices? The challenge is immense, demanding a multifaceted approach. We must acknowledge the pain caused by past injustices, actively work towards restorative justice, and promote policies that address root causes of inequality. This doesn't negate the importance of individual forgiveness; rather, it places it within a broader context of societal transformation. Forgiveness becomes a powerful tool for personal healing, while simultaneously informing our commitment to broader social justice.

Furthermore, the complexities of forgiveness become more nuanced when considering the scale of atrocities committed throughout history. The Holocaust, the Rwandan genocide, the Armenian genocide—these events represent such profound human suffering that the concept of forgiveness may seem inadequate, even offensive to those who have endured unimaginable loss.

Yet, the pursuit of justice and healing often involves a process of remembrance, reconciliation, and, ultimately, a search for a path forward that allows communities to rebuild and move towards a future of peace. Even in these instances, the act of forgiving, while not erasing the past, can become a powerful act of self-liberation, freeing individuals from the shackles of bitterness and hatred, allowing them to reclaim their lives and build a future free from the shadows of the past.

The path toward forgiveness and reconciliation is not a quick fix or a simple formula. It is a journey, often fraught with challenges, setbacks, and moments of doubt. It requires patience, perseverance, and a deep commitment to the transformative power of grace. It demands a willingness to engage with our own biases, confront our own complicity in systems of oppression, and actively work towards creating a more just and equitable world.

But the rewards of this journey are immeasurable: a society where fear is replaced with hope; where division is replaced with unity; and where the transformative power of faith fosters a culture of empathy, understanding, and love.

This is not merely a utopian ideal. It's a tangible goal, achieved through the conscious and diligent cultivation of forgiveness and reconciliation. It is the ultimate testament to our faith, a powerful reflection of the very nature of God who offers forgiveness and extends grace even to those who have deeply wronged us. When we embrace this divine nature, we can find the strength to transcend fear, build bridges of understanding, and create a world that truly reflects the Kingdom of God on earth.

Examples of forgiveness and reconciliation

Early Christians

Consider the historical context where the early church, born amidst the oppressive Roman Empire, found its strength not in conquest or retribution, but in the radical message of love and forgiveness. The early Christians, facing persecution and martyrdom, chose not to retaliate with violence. Their response was one of steadfast faith, unwavering in their belief in a God who forgives even the most egregious sins. This wasn't passive acceptance of oppression; it was a deliberate choice, a powerful statement that transcended the fear of earthly power.

Their unwavering commitment to forgiveness and reconciliation, even in the face of unimaginable suffering, became a testament to the transformative power of faith, demonstrating that even the most entrenched hatred can be overcome by grace. This historical example serves as a beacon, a reminder that even in the darkest of times, the light of forgiveness can pierce the shadows of fear and division.

Dietrich Bonhoeffer

Think of Dietrich Bonhoeffer, a Lutheran pastor who courageously resisted the Nazi regime. He understood the destructive nature of fear and hatred. His unwavering faith, coupled with his commitment to justice and reconciliation, led him to participate in the plot to assassinate Hitler. Although his actions ultimately resulted in his execution, his life and writings remain a powerful testament to the importance of resisting oppressive ideologies and striving for reconciliation.

Bonhoeffer's legacy serves as a stark reminder that true faith requires active engagement with the political realities of our time. It demands that we confront evil, even at personal cost, while simultaneously holding on to the hope of reconciliation. He understood that forgiveness wasn't about condoning evil, but about breaking the cycle of violence and hatred, paving the way for a more just and peaceful future.

Erika Kirk

Erika Kirk (née Frantzve) was married to Charlie Kirk, an evangelical Christian and a Christian conservative. As a Christian conservative, he sought to influence politics and public policy with the teachings of Christianity. He traveled extensively, visiting college campuses speaking to young people, converting many to Christianity. Charlie was fatally shot on September 10, 2025, while speaking at an Oregon university.

During a public and televised vigil on September 14, Erika forgave the gunman accused of killing him because that's what Jesus would want, stating that "The answer to hate is not hate. The answer we know from the Gospel is love and always love." Although the nature of Charlie's work is somewhat controversial, Christians are one body in Christ, and his Word shines above all else.

Chapter 12: Build a culture of faith over fear

The relentless barrage of fear-inducing narratives in today's political landscape can leave even the most steadfast believer feeling adrift.

We've examined how fear can be used as a tool, distorting truth and fostering divisive ideologies disguised as faith. To build a culture of genuine faith, we must not only acknowledge this issue but also develop spiritual resilience against it. This requires a deliberate engagement with spiritual disciplines, practices designed not just to soothe the soul, but to fortify it against the corrosive power of fear.

Think of the ancient spiritual traditions, practices honed over centuries to nurture inner peace and resilience. Consider the desert fathers and mothers, whose lives were shaped by periods of intense solitude and prayer. They weren't merely escaping the world but forging an inner strength, a spiritual muscle, which enabled them to face persecution and hardship with unwavering faith. Their discipline wasn't about avoidance but about empowerment. It was about cultivating an inner wellspring of strength, a reservoir of grace to draw upon when the storms of life raged. Jesus said it best when speaking to the Woman at the well:

> *"Everyone who drinks this water will be thirsty again, but whoever drinks the water I give them will never thirst. Indeed, the water I give them will become in them a spring of water welling up to eternal life."* (John 4:13-14).

A culture driven by faith instead of fear is essential for promoting justice, peace, and unity. Such a culture encourages individuals and communities to act with compassion, courage, and conviction, grounded in the principles of God's kingdom. Building this culture requires intentional efforts at levels of individuals, the Church, and the community.

Build oneself through spiritual disciplines

Building a culture of faith over fear begins with each individual. Practicing spiritual disciplines is a key factor in this process. Reading the Scriptures, praying, and meditating, as well as other disciplines, will help to ground you for building the culture within the Church and the community.

Pray

Prayer is one of the most fundamental spiritual disciplines. Not the rote recitation of memorized phrases, but a genuine, heartfelt conversation with God. It's about opening our hearts to His presence, laying bare our anxieties and fears, and allowing His peace to wash over us (Matthew 6:5-15, 25-34; Philippians 4:4-9). This isn't a passive activity; it requires intentional time and space, a deliberate setting aside of distractions to focus on the LORD. It involves wrestling with difficult questions, expressing doubts, and acknowledging our vulnerabilities. The process of honest prayer—laying our burdens at God's feet—is a powerful act of resilience-building.

Meditate

Meditation, a practice often associated with Eastern traditions, is not about emptying the mind but about focusing it, quieting the incessant chatter of our thoughts to create space for God's presence. Meditation might involve focusing on a specific Scripture, a repeated phrase, or simply the rhythm of one's breath while prayerfully acknowledging the presence of God. The practice cultivates a sense of stillness, an inner calm that provides a counterpoint to the frenetic energy of the world around us. It strengthens our ability to discern truth from falsehood and to remain grounded amidst chaos.

Fast

The potent spiritual discipline of fasting is often misunderstood as mere self-denial. It's not just about abstaining from food; it's about spiritual reflection and deepening one's dependence on God. By temporarily denying ourselves physical gratification, we create a heightened awareness of our spiritual needs and deepen our reliance on divine sustenance. Fasting can be a powerful tool for breaking free from unhealthy attachments, including the attachment to power, control, and the validation that often fuels political engagement based on fear. It allows us to see our dependence on God more clearly, empowering us to face difficult realities with greater faith.

Read Scripture

Scripture reading and study provide another crucial pathway to resilience. Engaging with the Bible isn't merely about intellectual understanding; it's about allowing God's word to penetrate our hearts and transform our perspectives. It involves reflecting on stories of faith and perseverance, drawing strength from the struggles and triumphs of those who have gone before us. It offers a framework for understanding suffering, injustice, and the complexities of human nature. This engagement isn't passive; it requires careful study, contemplation, and prayerful reflection. It requires wrestling with challenging passages, allowing them to challenge our assumptions and expand our understanding of God's character and purposes.

Rest on Sabbath

The practice of Sabbath rest is often overlooked in our relentlessly busy lives. It is more than a day off; it is a sacred pause, a time to disconnect from the relentless demands of work and the constant bombardment of information, to reconnect with God and with ourselves. It's a chance to cultivate gratitude for God's gifts, to renew our strength, and to approach our lives and engagement with the world with a refreshed perspective. This practice actively combats the anxiety and depletion that can easily arise from constant engagement with fear-inducing news cycles and political discourse.

Cultivate a sense of community

Beyond these individual disciplines, cultivating a strong sense of community is essential. The church, when functioning as it should, is a place of refuge, a sanctuary where we can find support, encouragement, and accountability. It's a place to share our burdens, to celebrate our triumphs, and to learn from one another. Strong community helps us resist the isolating effects of fear, reminding us that we are not alone in our struggles. It fosters a sense of belonging and shared purpose, providing strength and resilience in the face of adversity.

Develop a theology of hope

Developing a theology of hope is crucial in countering the pervasive influence of fear. This isn't simply blind optimism; it's a deep-seated trust in God's sovereignty and goodness, a conviction that even amidst suffering and injustice, God is working towards His purposes. It involves embracing the promise of God's grace and believing that He is present even in the darkest of times. A theology of hope enables us to engage with difficult realities without succumbing to despair, offering a framework for understanding suffering within the larger context of God's redemptive plan.

Embrace vulnerability and empathy

Finally, embracing vulnerability and empathy is of paramount importance. Fear often thrives on division and dehumanization. By choosing vulnerability, by openly acknowledging our own imperfections and uncertainties, we create space for authentic connection with others. Empathy, the ability to understand and share the feelings of others, allows us to bridge political divides and build relationships across differing viewpoints. It fosters an atmosphere of mutual respect and understanding, weakening the power of fear-mongering narratives that rely on others and demonizing those who hold different opinions.

Build a culture within the church

The path to building a culture of faith that transcends fear is not a passive one; it demands intentionality, discipline, and a profound commitment to nurturing our spiritual well-being. It is a lifelong journey that requires consistent effort and a willingness to embrace the practices that foster resilience and inner peace. By actively engaging in these spiritual disciplines, we not only equip ourselves to resist the power of fear but also become agents of hope and reconciliation in a world desperately in need of both. The result will be a stronger, more resilient faith—one that is not easily swayed by political manipulation and is actively engaged in building a more just and compassionate world.

The solitary struggle against fear is a losing battle. While personal spiritual disciplines provide a crucial inner fortitude, they are most potent when interwoven with the strength and support of a vibrant, faith-filled community. This is not merely a matter of social comfort; it is a fundamental theological and practical necessity. Our faith, after all, is not meant to be lived in isolation. It is inherently relational, echoing the Trinitarian nature of God—a communion of persons bound together in love. To isolate oneself spiritually is to diminish the very essence of what it means to be Christian.

The early church, persecuted and marginalized, thrived not despite its communal structure, but because of it. The Acts of the Apostles vividly portrays a community of Christ followers that were bound together by shared faith, mutual support, and a radical commitment to one another. They shared their resources, cared for the vulnerable, and faced persecution with courage that stemmed from their collective strength. Their example serves as a powerful reminder of the profound resilience that emerges when believers stand shoulder to shoulder, sharing burdens and offering encouragement. Imagine the early Christians huddled in their hidden meeting places, sharing not only bread but also stories of faith, prayer, and hope in the face of unimaginable adversity. Their courage was not born of individual strength alone, but of a shared faith and mutual encouragement, bolstering each other's spirits in the darkest of times.

This communal aspect is echoed throughout Christian history. Consider the monastic communities of the Middle Ages, finding solace and strength in shared prayer, rigorous discipline, and mutual accountability. Their lives, lived in intentional community, demonstrated the power of collective support in overcoming personal struggles and pursuing spiritual growth. The communal aspect of monastic life was not merely a matter of convenience; it was essential to their spiritual well-being. They understood that the journey of faith is not a solitary trek but a shared pilgrimage, where each member supports and encourages the others. The vibrant spiritual life that characterized these communities can't be attributed to individual piety alone; it was the fruit of a life lived in intentional interdependence.

The same principle applies to the modern church. A healthy congregation is not simply a collection of individuals attending services; it is a living organism, where members are interconnected, supporting one another in times of joy and sorrow (Romans 12; 1 Corinthians 12; Ephesians 4; Philippians 2:4; and 1 Peter 1-4). It is a place where vulnerability is embraced, where burdens are shared, and where individuals find strength and encouragement in their faith journey. The absence of a supportive community can leave believers isolated, vulnerable to the manipulation of fear-mongering narratives, and ultimately, spiritually depleted.

The importance of community extends beyond emotional support. It provides a crucial check against the spread of misinformation and conspiracy theories, often fueled by fear. Within a thriving community, believers can engage in discerning conversations, critically examining information, and grounding their beliefs in Scripture and theological tradition. A strong community fosters a culture of intellectual honesty and mutual accountability, preventing the spread of falsehoods and extremist ideologies that often thrive in isolation.

This is particularly crucial in navigating the complex political landscape of our times. The echo chambers of social media, coupled with the divisive rhetoric of contemporary politics, can easily isolate individuals and leave them susceptible to fear-based narratives. Within a healthy community, however, believers can engage in thoughtful discussions, wrestle with difficult questions, and find common ground amidst differing perspectives. They can learn from one another, challenge one another's assumptions, and work together to develop informed and faith-based responses to political issues.

Consider the example of churches actively involved in social justice initiatives. These congregations often provide a crucial support network for marginalized communities, offering not only spiritual guidance but also practical assistance. They act as a bulwark against fear, offering hope and empowerment to those who feel marginalized and oppressed. Their work is a powerful testament to the transformative power of a faith-filled community actively engaged in building a more just and compassionate world.

Building this kind of supportive community requires intentional effort. It necessitates a commitment to fostering genuine relationships, actively listening to one another's concerns, and creating a space where vulnerability is embraced, not condemned. This requires a move away from individualism towards a genuine commitment to interconnectedness, recognizing that each member of the community is essential to its overall well-being. It means actively working to create inclusive spaces, where individuals from diverse backgrounds feel welcomed, valued, and respected.

The creation of a supportive community is not merely a social endeavor; it is a spiritual imperative. It mirrors the very essence of the Triune God, a community of persons bound together in love and mutual support. By actively cultivating this communal aspect of our faith, we not only fortify ourselves against the corrosive power of fear but also become agents of hope and transformation in a world desperately in need of both. It is through this communal support, this shared journey of faith, that we can truly build a culture of faith that transcends fear, creating a world where love conquers fear, and hope triumphs over despair.

The work of building such a community is ongoing, requiring constant nurturing, vigilance, and a deep commitment to the principles of faith, love, and justice. It is a challenging yet rewarding endeavor, one that leads to a richer, more meaningful, and more resilient faith. The strength we draw from this community, grounded in the love of Christ, becomes an unstoppable force for good in a world desperately seeking hope and reconciliation. This collaborative effort, this shared faith journey, is the bedrock upon which a culture of faith that transcends fear is built and sustained.

Build a culture within the community

Intentional community building within the church needs to extend beyond the walls of the church building. We are called to be ambassadors of Christ in the world, engaging with others who hold different perspectives, even those who are opposed to our beliefs. This engagement must be rooted in love, compassion, and a commitment to truth-seeking, but it also requires the support and encouragement of our community. This engagement should never be approached alone but through the framework of a support system that will bolster you and help you stay grounded.

Sharing stories within the community is also vital. The sharing of personal struggles, triumphs, and the ways in which faith has helped navigate difficult times, builds empathy and understanding within the community. When individuals share their vulnerabilities, they create a space for others to do the same, fostering a sense of shared humanity and breaking down the barriers of isolation. This shared vulnerability strengthens the bonds of the community and cultivates a deeper sense of belonging and mutual support.

The community provides a space for spiritual growth. Through shared prayer, Bible studies, and fellowship, individuals can deepen their understanding of God's word and grow in their faith journey. This shared exploration of faith strengthens the individual believer and fortifies the community. The community becomes a crucible for spiritual growth, where individuals are challenged, supported, and inspired to live out their faith in the world.

In addition to spiritual growth, community can act as a powerful force for social change. When believers come together, they can leverage their collective resources and influence to address injustice and advocate for positive change in the world. This collective action amplifies their voices and increases their impact on the broader society, empowering them to challenge the systems and structures that perpetuate fear and oppression.

Finally, the community offers refuge from the pressures of the world, a space where individuals can find rest, renewal, and encouragement in their faith journey. This sanctuary provides a vital counterpoint to the anxieties and uncertainties of daily life, providing strength and resilience to face the challenges that lie ahead. It is within this supportive community that the individual believer can find the strength to overcome fear and live a life of faith, hope, and love.

Building upon the bedrock of community, we now ascend to a higher plane: the cultivation of a robust theology of hope. This is not mere optimism, a Pollyannish refusal to acknowledge suffering. Rather, it is a deeply theological conviction rooted in the very nature of God, a conviction that transcends the ephemeral anxieties of the present and anchors itself in the eternal promises of the future. It's a hope that isn't naïve; it acknowledges the darkness, the injustice, the suffering that permeates our world. Yet, it refuses to be consumed by it.

Scriptural insights on building a faith-driven culture

The Bible provides guidance on building a culture of faith over fear. Jesus tells His followers,

> *"You are the light of the world. A town built on a hill cannot be hidden. Neither do people light a lamp and put it under a bowl. Instead, they put it on its stand, and it gives light to everyone in the house. In the same way, let your light shine before others, that they may see your good deeds and glorify your Father in heaven."* (Matthew 5:14-16).

This passage calls for believers to be a visible and positive presence in the world, reflecting God's light through their actions. Building a faith-driven culture involves being a witness to God's love, justice, and peace in every aspect of life.

Theological reflections on community and culture

Theologically, the church is called to be a counter-cultural community that reflects the values of God's kingdom. This involves living out the principles of love, justice, and peace in a world often driven by fear and division. The early Christian communities in Acts 2 and 4 provide a model of communal living that embodies these values.

The concept of the "Kingdom of God" is central to this vision. The Kingdom of God is not just a future reality but a present one that believers are called to live out. This involves challenging the existing norms and working towards a society that reflects God's righteousness and justice.

Examples of communities embracing faith over fear

Consider the following communities that embraced faith over fear by choosing love, purpose, and growth:

- **The Quakers and peace advocacy.** The Religious Society of Friends, commonly known as Quakers, have a long history of advocating peace and justice. Their commitment to nonviolence and equality is grounded in their faith, and they have been involved in numerous movements for social change.
- **L'Arche communities.** Founded by Jean Vanier, L'Arche communities bring together people with and without intellectual disabilities to live and work together. These communities exemplify a culture of acceptance, love, and faith, challenging societal fears and prejudices.
- **The Sanctuary Movement.** The Sanctuary Movement provided protection and support to refugees fleeing violence. This movement was driven by a commitment to justice and compassion, rooted in faith.

How to build a faith-driven culture

Use the following guidelines to build a faith-driven culture:

- **Promote positive narratives.** Share stories of faith, courage, and hope that inspire others to overcome fear. Highlight examples of individuals and communities making a positive impact.

- **Encourage critical thinking.** Equip individuals with the skills to critically evaluate information and resist fearmongering. This can involve educational programs, workshops, and discussions.

- **Foster community engagement.** Create opportunities to promote positive narratives and for community members to engage in meaningful actions that address fear-driven issues. This can include service projects, advocacy campaigns, interfaith dialogues, and even community events.

- **Celebrate diversity.** Embrace and celebrate the diversity within your community. Encourage mutual respect and understanding, and work towards inclusive policies and practices.

- **Practice persistent prayer.** Commit to regular prayer for your community and its leaders. Seek God's guidance and strength in building a culture of faith over fear.

Appendix A: Reflections and discussion questions

1. Reflect on a time when you experienced fear related to a political issue. How did it impact your thoughts and actions?

2. What are some examples of how fear is used in current political discourse?

3. Consider how Paul demonstrated faith in the face of fear. How can his example inspire you in your political engagement?

4. What's a good way to foster a respectful and constructive dialogue with someone who has different political views?

5. When has your faith helped you overcome a fearful situation? How did it change your perspective and actions?

6. Identify a current political issue that causes fear in your community. How can you respond with faith and advocacy for justice?

7. When has fear influenced your perception of a particular group or issue? How did you overcome it?

8. Read 1 John 4:18. How does this speak to overcoming fear and division, and how can it be applied in your context?

9. What is the role of personal faith in overcoming political fear, and how can your faith guide your actions and responses?

10. Identify a historical or contemporary figure who exemplifies courage in the face of political fear. What can you learn from their example?

11. In 1 Peter 2, Peter writes that Christians are "strangers and aliens." What insights does this provide about the ways that followers of Jesus Christ join in cultural discussions?

12. How do the writings of the prophets Amos, Micah, and Jonah inform us concerning themes of justice, humility, and compassion in engaging our neighbors in society?

13. Consider how the following Biblical characters demonstrated courage in the face of political fear. What can you learn from their examples?
    - Esther and Mordecai
    - Daniel
    - Shadrach, Meshach, and Abednego
    - Stephen

Appendix B: Scripture reference

Preface

Genesis 1:26	Matthew 11:28:16-20	Matthew 11:22-37-39

Chapter 1. Introduction

Matthew 22:37-39	John 10:10	2 Timothy 2:11–13
Revelation 13:17	Romans 8:18-28	2 Timothy 1:7
Psalm 46:1	2 Corinthians 1:3-4	Jonah 4
Revelation 13:17	2 Timothy 1:7	Matthew 5:24-27
Jonah 1-4	Acts 19:26-28	Matthew 5-7
John 16:33	2 Timothy 4:14	

Chapter 2. The politics of fear

Matthew 5:16-17	2 Timothy 1:7	Matthew 10:28
Matthew 28:16-20	Matthew 7:24-25	1 Samuel 17
John 16:33	Isaiah 41:10	

Chapter 3. Address scapegoating and embrace diversity

1 Timothy 6	Deuteronomy 10:12-22	John 14:27
Romans 12:2	Deuteronomy 10:18-19	Hebrews 11
Galatians 3:28	Joshua 1:9	Isaiah 1:17

Chapter 4. The impact of political fear on society

Acts 2:42-47	1 John 4:18	Acts 7:54-60
1 Corinthians 12	Isaiah 41:10	
Ephesians 2:14-16	Isaiah 41:13	

Chapter 5. Christian nationalism: When faith becomes political power

Joshua 1:9

Chapter 6. Christian nationalism: Dangers of idolatry

Jeremiah 2:11-13	Romans 1:20-23	Matthew 5:44
Matthew 28:20	Romans 3:23	Romans 13:1-7
Genesis 12:1-4	Matthew 22:37-39	Matthew 5-7
Acts 17:26	Luke 10:25-37	Luke 10:25-37
Revelations 7	John 18:36	

Chapter 7. The role of Christians in addressing political fear

Acts 2:42-47	Micah 6:8	Matthew 6:25-34
Philippians 3:20	1 Peter 1:3–9	Micah 6:8
1 John 4:18	Ephesians 6:10-18	Matthew 25:31-46

Chapter 8. Conspiracy theories and the Christian response

1 Corinthians 14:33	Psalm 119:105	Matthew 5:9
Proverbs 3:5-6	Proverbs 3:5–6	Philippians 2:1–2
John 8:44	1 Thessalonians 5:21	Isaiah 41:10

Chapter 9. A Christian response to fears of disease and death

2 Kings 5	John 14:1–3	Psalm 46:1–2
Matthew 8:1–4	Hebrews 2:14–15	Romans 8:38–39
Luke 17:11–19	Psalm 23	Revelation 21:4

Chapter 10. Fear of government corruption

Exodus 1:9-10	Psalm 99

Chapter 11. Cultivate hope, empathy, and forgiveness

Micah 6:8	Romans 8:28	Luke 10:30-37

Chapter 12. Build a culture of faith over fear

John 4:13-14	1 Corinthians 12	1 Peter 1-4
Matthew 6:5-15, 25-34	Ephesians 4	Matthew 5:14-16
Philippians 4:4-9	Philippians 2:4	Acts 2 and 4
Romans 12		

Glossary

Note: *The following terms can carry different connotations and interpretations depending on the context and the perspective of the person using them. While some may employ them as objective labels, others may use them in a derogatory or inflammatory manner to discredit or attack opposing viewpoints*

antifa

A left-wing anti-fascist and anti-racist political movement in the United States. It consists of a highly decentralized array of autonomous groups that achieve their aims either through nonviolent direct action or violence.

antifascist

An activist or protestor who opposes fascist rule or movements. Antifascists employ a range of tactics, from peaceful protests and speeches to more confrontational or violent actions aimed at countering fascism.

autocrat

A ruler with unlimited political, economic, social, and military power.

authoritarianism

A political philosophy and type of government rule where a singular person or political party holds all power. The government uses fear and violence to divide and rule.

Christian nationalism

The merging of Christian cultural and national identities, addressing the perspectives of its followers, to attain significance or influence in political, cultural, and social spheres.

Civil Rights Movement

The historic struggle for racial equality and social justice in the United States, primarily led by African Americans in the mid-20th century. Key figures include Martin Luther King Jr., Rosa Parks, John Lewis, James Farmer, Fannie Lou Hamer, Ella Baker, James Baldwin, Cesar Chavez, and Paul Robeson. This movement used nonviolent resistance and civil disobedience to advocate equal rights and end discriminatory laws and practices.

conspiracy theory

An unproven explanation for an event or phenomenon, often involving accusations of secret plots or cover-ups by powerful individuals or groups. While some elements of conspiracy theories may be true, they generally lack verifiable evidence and are based on speculation and circumstantial evidence.

Critical Race Theory (CRT)

An academic framework that examines the role of race and racism in society, particularly within legal and institutional systems. Originally a course of study in law schools, CRT has become a controversial topic, with critics accusing it of promoting divisiveness and Marxist ideologies, while supporters view it as essential for understanding and addressing systemic racism.

curse of Ham

A misnomer referring to a curse from Noah to Ham's son, Canaan, when Ham saw Noah drunk and uncovered in his tent. (Genesis 9: 20-27). In the 18th and 19th centuries, this was misconstrued in a way to justify the enslavement of Black people: Ham was cursed; dark skin was part of the curse; and his descendants were African. None of those interpretations are Scripturally sound.

fascist

A supporter of fascism, an authoritarian ultra-nationalistic political ideology characterized by centralized power, forcible suppression of opposition, and strong emphasis on national unity and racial or ethnic superiority.

Great Replacement Theory

A conspiracy theory adopted by the white supremacist movement stating that immigration policies welcoming nonwhite immigrants are part of a plot designed to replace the political power, undermine the culture of white people living in Western countries, and even destroy the white race altogether.

idol

Something other than God that becomes an object of profound admiration or devotion.

Ku Klux Klan (KKK)

A vigilante group that was founded in 1865 as a direct response to the South's defeat in the Civil War. It's a Protestant-led extremist, white supremacist, far-right hate group. The members employ terror in pursuit of their white supremacist goals.

leftist

A term often used pejoratively to describe individuals or groups perceived as holding liberal, progressive, or left-leaning political views, typically associated with the Democratic Party in the United States.

Marxist

A follower of the political and economic theories of Karl Marx, which advocate for the abolition of private property and the establishment of a classless society through revolutionary struggle between the working class and the capitalist class. Marxism often includes an atheistic worldview and focuses on materialism.

Nazi

A member or supporter of the German fascist party led by Adolf Hitler in Germany during the 1930s and 1940s. Nazis promoted extreme nationalism, racism, and antisemitism, and were responsible for the Holocaust and other atrocities during World War II.

Oath Keepers

A far-right militia that was incorporated in 2009 by Elmer Rhodes, a former paratrooper and lawyer. Its leaders were convicted of violently opposing the government of the United States during the 2021 attempted coup, including the transfer of presidential power as prescribed by the United States constitution.

political fear

The fear caused by political systems or authorities through violence, repression, exclusion, or propaganda, aimed at influencing behavior and suppressing opposition.

114

Proud Boys

Established in 2016, a neofascist white nationalist organization that promotes and engages in political violence. Its leaders were convicted of violently opposing the government of the United States during the 2021 attempted coup, including the transfer of presidential power as prescribed by the United States constitution.

racist

Someone who holds prejudiced beliefs or exhibits discriminatory behavior toward individuals or groups based on their race or ethnicity. Racism can manifest in various forms, including overt acts of hatred, subtle micro-aggressions, or systemic biases embedded within institutions and societal structures.

right-wing

Refers to conservative or reactionary political views, typically associated with support for traditional values, limited government intervention, and strong emphasis on patriotism and nationalism. Some right-wing segments are accused of promoting nationalism that despises the poor, Blacks, and people of different nationalities, focusing on issues like the unborn and marriage.

Sanctuary Movement

A campaign in the United States started in the early 1980s to provide safe haven for Central American refugees fleeing civil conflict. This movement was a response to federal immigration policies that made obtaining asylum challenging for Central Americans.

scapegoat

A person or group who gets unfairly blamed for problems in society. Leaders use scapegoats to make people afraid of someone else, so they don't look too closely at the real issues or who's truly responsible. It's a way to distract, divide, and control people through fear.

woke

Originally used to describe awareness and active attention to issues of racial and social injustice. In conservative political and evangelical circles, it is often used pejoratively to criticize an over-focus on social issues or the "social gospel." Conversely, in larger theological and political circles, it is affirmed as being aware of injustices, such as police brutality, exemplified by cases like George Floyd, Breonna Taylor, and Trayvon Martin.

Bibliography

"America's Top 10 Fears: The 2021 American Fear Index." *Safehome.org*, https://www.safehome.org/home-safety/american-fear-study/. Accessed 29 Dec. 2022.

Barna, George. American Worldview Inventory 2021-22: The Annual Report on the State of Worldview in the United States. Arizona Christian University Press, 2022.

Bell, Derrick A. "Who's Afraid of Critical Race Theory?" *Who's Afraid of Critical Race Theory?*, vol. 1995, no. 4, University of Illinois Law Review, 1995, pp. 893–910.

Catalini, Mike, et al. "Trump Falsely Accuses Immigrants in Ohio of Abducting and Eating Pets." *AP News*, 11 Sept. 2024, https://apnews.com/article/haitian-immigrants-vance-trump-ohio-6e4a47c52b23ae2c802d216369512ca5.

Drew, Charles D. Body Broken: Can Republicans and Democrats Sit in the Same Pew? 2nd ed., New Growth Press, 2012.

Engels, Friedrich, and Karl Marx. *The Communist Manifesto*. Penguin Classics, 2015.

Fea, John. *Believe Me: The Evangelical Road to Donald Trump*. William B Eerdmans Publishing, 2018.

Foxe, John, and The Voice of the Martyrs. *Foxe: Voices of the Martyrs: Ad33 - Today*. Salem Books, 2019.

Grenz, Stanley J., and Roger E. Olson. *20th Century Theology: God and the World in a Transitional Age*. Send The Light, 1993.

Gonçalves, Lara Sartorio. "The politics of fear and the authoritarian political imagination." *Isa-sociology.org*, https://globaldialogue.isa-sociology.org/articles/the-politics-of-fear-and-the-authoritarian-political-imagination. Accessed 10 Nov. 2024.

Grevin, Christian. *The Top 10 Fears in America 2022 - Did your fears make the list?* The Voice of Wilkinson. Retrieved April 8, 2023, from https://blogs.chapman.edu/wilkinson/2022/10/14/the-top-10-fears-in-america-2022/.

Hitler, Adolf. *Mein Kampf*. Pimlico, 1992.

Isichei, Elizabeth. A History of Christianity in Africa: From Antiquity to the Present. SPCK Publishing, 1995.

Lawson, Steven J. *Pillars of Grace: A.D. 100-1564*. Ligonier Ministries, 2011.

Longman, Tremper, III. The Bible and the Ballot: Using Scripture in Political Decisions. Wm. B. Eerdmans Publishing Co., 2022.

Miller, Chris. "Deseret News Archives: World First Learns of Adolf Hitler from 1923 'Beer-Hall Putsch.'" *Deseret News Salt Lake City, Utah: 1964)*, Deseret News, 8 Nov. 2024, https://www.deseret.com/utah/2024/11/08/deseret-news-archives-world-learns-of-adolf-hitler-from-1923-beer-hall-putsch/.

Montanaro, Domenico. "Hillary Clinton's 'basket of Deplorables,' in Full Context of This Ugly Campaign." *NPR*, NPR, 10 Sept. 2016, https://www.npr.org/2016/09/10/493427601/hillary-clintons-basket-of-deplorables-in-full-context-of-this-ugly-campaign.

Mundell, E. 2024, November 7. Rates of Anxiety, Depression Rising Among Americans.

Especially the Young. Usnews.com. https://www.usnews.com/news/health-news/articles/2024-11-07/rates-of-anxiety-depression-rising-among-americans-especially-the-young.

"Nazi Germany." Americanhistory.si.edu, https://americanhistory.si.edu/explore/exhibitions/price-of-freedom/online/world-war-ii/axis-aggression/nazi-germany. Accessed 10 Nov. 2024.

Olson, Roger E. The Story of Christian Theology: Twenty Centuries of Tradition and Reform. Apollos, 1999.

Onion, Amanda. "Adolf Hitler: Rise to Power, Impact & Death." *HISTORY*, 29 Oct. 2009, https://www.history.com/topics/world-war-ii/adolf-hitler-1.

Principles and Purposes of the Knights of the Ku Klux Klan Are Outlined by an Exalted Cyclops of the Order. *Yale.edu*, https://collections.library.yale.edu/catalog/16173379?child_oid=16173608. Accessed 5 Sept. 2024.

Perkins, John M., and Priscilla Perkins. *Let Justice Roll Down.* Baker Books, 2021.

Ramet, S. P. 1998). Nihil Obstat: Religion, Politics, and Social Change in East-Central Europe and Russia. Duke University Press. Ray, Siladitya. "'They're Eating the Dogs' and 'Worst' Inflation: Key Fact-Checks from the Presidential Debate." *Forbes*, 11 Sept. 2024, https://www.forbes.com/sites/siladityaray/2024/09/11/theyre-eating-the-cats-and-worst-inflation-key-fact-checks-from-the-presidential-debate/.

"Tertullian: 'The Blood of the Martyrs Is the Seed of the Church.'" *The Socratic Method*, 8 Nov. 2023, https://www.socratic-method.com/quote-meanings/tertullian-the-blood-of-the-martyrs-is-the-seed-of-the-church.

"The Edict of Milan - Lactantius." *Earlychurchtexts.com*, https://earlychurch-texts.com/public/edict_of_milan.htm. Accessed 11 Nov. 2024.

Tyler, A., Whitehead, A., Perry, S., Butler, A., Tisby, J., Stewart, K., & Seidel, A. L. n.d.).

Attack on the capitol: Evidence of the role of white Christian nationalism. Bjconline.org. Retrieved April 22, 2023, from https://bjconline.org/wp-content/uploads/2022/02/Christian_Nationalism_and_the_Jan6_Insurrection-2-9-22.pdf.

Uggerud, Kristoffer. "The Early Christian Martyrs: Persecutions in the Roman Empire."

The Collector, 10 June 2023, https://www.thecollector.com/early-christian-martyrs/.

Waldroff, Kirk. "Fear: A Powerful Motivator in Elections." *American Psychological Association*, 13 Oct. 2020, https://www.apa.org/news/apa/2020/fear-motivator-elections.

Washington, Booker T. *Up from Slavery.* Signet Classics, 2010.

"What Were Joseph Stalin's Goals as World War Two Ended." *Dailyhistory.org*, https://www.dailyhistory.org/What_were_Joseph_Stalin's_goals_as_World_War_Two_ended. Accessed 10 Nov. 2024.

White, James Emery. The Rise of the Nones: Understanding and Reaching the Religiously Unaffiliated. Baker Books, 2014.

Winter, Ralph D., and Steven C. Hawthorne, editors. *Perspectives on the World Christian Movement 4th Ed): A Reader.* 4th ed., William Carey Library, 2020.

Wurmbrand, Richard. *Tortured for Christ.* Zondervan, 1992.

Wurmbrand, R. 1998). Tortured for Christ. Living Sacrifice Book Co.

About the Author

Charles Clemons is a chaplain, author, and leadership development professional whose ministry bridges faith, social awareness, and emotional resilience. A former youth and lead pastor serving both African American and multiethnic congregations, he has also worked internationally in Christian relief and development initiatives across Africa. Today, Charles serves as a full-time hospital chaplain at UCLA Medical Center, where he provides compassionate support to families in crisis.

As the founder of Charles Clemons LLC, he produces leadership training, mentorship programs, and The On-Purpose Leader Podcast, inspiring others to live and lead with faith, purpose, and moral courage. His writing blends biblical insight with historical reflection, speaking to the challenges and hopes of our time.

www.ingramcontent.com/pod-product-compliance
Lightning Source LLC
Chambersburg PA
CBHW031213270326
41931CB00006B/547